I0605555

GOAL!

AWESOME SOCCER STORIES AND FUN FACTS FOR KIDS

CARLOS MOJICA

becker&mayer! kids

AFA
10
10

CONTENTS

Lionel Messi of Argentina kicks the ball during the FIFA World Cup Qatar 2022.

AIRWAYS
30

Introduction

Soccer has a long and rich history of players who have captured the public's imagination and the hearts of soccer supporters everywhere. The history of the sport is so fascinating, and its impact on the world so massive, that there are universities that teach entire classes about soccer. While you may not be enrolled in university just yet, you can think of this book as a fun class on the greats who have played the beautiful game, which makes you a student of the game.

This book explores the origins of soccer, explains how it's played, breaks down each position and its role, and features a list of players from around the world along with the teams they've played for and their accolades. While this book is not a full list of the great players in the sport (that would take forever!), it does include some of the most legendary names—and some cool ones you may not know about yet! You may find some of your favorite players featured in these pages or find some new favorites.

As you read this book, think about the players that inspire you: Who do you want to play like? More importantly, which players do you wish you could play with? You might find yourself talking about players from countries you've never visited or imagining what it would be like to play on a team with legends.

Much like soccer brings joy to the world, the hope is that this book strengthens your love for the sport. If you're completely new to soccer, then hopefully by the time you read the last page, you'll have a better understanding of it and the amazing players that play the game. My hope is that you'll have learned enough to fall in love with it the way so many of us around the world have.

Leo Messi of Paris Saint-Germain and Cristiano Ronaldo of Riyadh XI fight for possession during a friendly match at King Fahd International Stadium in 2023.

adidas

Chapter 1

A Global Passion

Imagine you're at a huge soccer game with tons of people, and you see a player kick the ball into the goal—just past the goalkeeper. GOAAAL! Everyone jumps up, cheers loudly, and starts chanting the player's name!

This scene vividly captures the passion that soccer ignites in people. What's even cooler is that you can play soccer anywhere in the world. Whether you call it soccer, football, *calcio*, *fútbol*, or *futebol*, this sport is worldwide and stirs the most intense emotions among its fans.

But what is soccer? It's a sport where two teams try to kick a ball into each other's net to score goals. The team with the most goals wins (see page 11).

In 1863, soccer had become so popular that England formed the Football Association (FA) to create rules that everyone could follow called the Laws of the Game. These rules allowed teams from different English clubs to play fair games against each other. By the 1900s, soccer had become popular enough that it became part of the Summer Olympics, with teams from England, France, and Belgium competing for gold medals.

Soon, people realized they needed a group to organize soccer games between countries, so FIFA (*Fédération Internationale de Football Association*, or International

QUICK KICKS

Where did soccer come from?

Although there is evidence of ancient civilizations playing games that involve kicking a ball—such as the Chinese, Greeks, and Romans—soccer, as we know it, originated in England. Over time, what started as a series of games that involved kicking and throwing a ball in England slowly developed into different sports, including rugby, (American) football, and, of course, soccer.

Iker Casillas, former captain of Spain

Federation of Association Football) was created in 1904 with seven nations as members. By 1930, the organization had forty members and was ready to hold its own international tournament: the FIFA World Cup.

Today, FIFA's membership includes 211 countries, all eligible to compete in the FIFA World Cup. What is the World Cup? It's an international championship held every four years to determine the best national team in the world. The World Cup is the sport's most prestigious competition and the most-watched sporting event globally.

> **QUICK KICKS**
>
> **The 2022 FIFA World Cup in Qatar had about 5 billion people watching—that's almost everyone in the world! The final match had a whopping 1.5 billion viewers—that's over 15,000 packed football fields.**

Beyond the World Cup, soccer is beloved because, at its core, it's a sport that can be played anywhere. After all, all you really need is a ball. For over a century, children and adults alike have played soccer anywhere you can think of—grass fields, dirt fields, concrete courts, asphalt streets, and even the beach. This is why soccer is called "the world's game."

Goal Getters

FIFA's Founders

Who were the seven founding nations who shaped the game?

- **FRANCE:** FIFA was born in Paris, France, in 1904. France also hosted two World Cups—one in 1938 and another in 1998, winning its first World Cup in 1998 at home against Brazil. France won the World Cup again in 2018, making them strong competitors in the sport.
- **BELGIUM:** Belgium's team is super popular, and they're called "The Red Devils." Their team's name goes back all the way to 1906. Along with France, Belgium was the other founding FIFA nation to play in the first World Cup in 1930.
- **DENMARK:** Denmark surprised everyone by winning a big soccer tournament called the European Championship in 1992—even though they weren't supposed to be in the tournament at first! They first qualified to play in the World Cup in 1986.
- **NETHERLANDS:** The Netherlands is famous for their creative soccer style called "Total Football," and they've been close to winning the World Cup three times! Their national team is nicknamed "*Oranje*" because of their orange uniforms.
- **SPAIN:** Spain has an awesome way of playing called "tiki-taka," which helped them win the World Cup in 2010. Tiki-taka is a style of play that focuses on possession and quick, short passes. Soccer is the most popular sport in Spain, and Spain houses two of the biggest clubs in soccer: Real Madrid and Barcelona.
- **SWEDEN:** Sweden hosted the World Cup once in 1958 and made it all the way to the final game! They have played in twelve FIFA World Cups since 1934, and their best results were in 1958 when they won second place.
- **SWITZERLAND:** Switzerland is where FIFA's headquarters are currently located. Similarly to Sweden, Switzerland has played in twelve World Cups since 1934. They set records for the longest time without conceding a goal in World Cup history with 559 minutes.

Soccer Organizations

Because soccer is played all around the world, different continents have their own groups called confederations that organize fun tournaments where different national teams can compete. These groups act as referees for whole regions—they make sure everything is fair and exciting.

Europe has the Union of European Football Associations (UEFA), which runs the Euro with the top European nations playing for a shiny trophy. South America has the Confederación Sudamericana de Fútbol (CONMEBOL), which hosts the Copa América. Africa's games are managed by the Confederation of African Football (CAF), known for the Africa Cup of Nations.

Over in Asia, the Asian Football Confederation (AFC) organizes the Asian Cup with amazing teams from places like Japan, India, and South Korea. North and Central America, plus the Caribbean, have the Confederation of North, Central America and Caribbean Association Football (Concacaf), which runs the Gold Cup. The islands of Oceania are guided by the Oceania Football Confederation (OFC), with tournaments like the OFC Nations Cup. And at the top of them all is of course FIFA—the global boss of soccer.

QUICK KICKS

In addition to hosting competitions, confederations also organize continental club tournaments.

AFC
Champions League Elite

CAF
Champions League

CONCACAF
Champions Cup

CONMEBOL
Copa Libertadores

OFC
Champions League

UEFA
Champions League, formerly European Cup

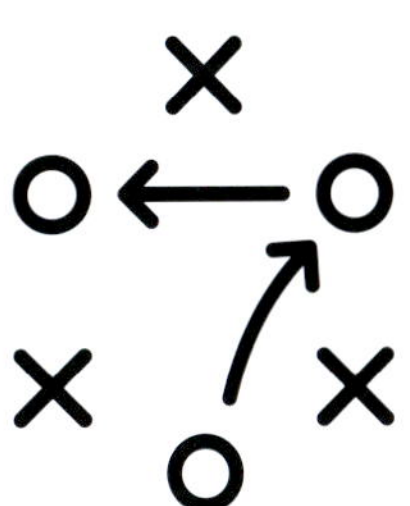

The Laws of the Game

Now that you know a little bit about what soccer is and where it came from, let's dive into the Laws of the Game.

- **TEAMS AND PLAYERS:** Soccer matches are played between two teams. Each soccer team has eleven eligible players (players allowed on the field at one time). Players can use their feet, head, and chest to move the ball, but only the goalkeeper, who protects the goal, gets to use their hands.
- **THE FIELD:** Soccer is played on a big, rectangular field called a regulation-sized field. It's usually 100 to 130 yards long and 50 to 100 yards wide.
- **SUBSTITUTIONS:** Sometimes, a player is replaced due to injury, strategy, or tiredness. Each team can make up to five substitutions during a match. Players who leave the field cannot come back in.
- **GAME DURATION:** The game is split into two halves, each lasting forty-five minutes.
- **SCORING GOALS:** Goals are scored by getting the ball into the other team's net, which is between two tall posts with a bar across the top. At the end of regulation time, the team with the most goals wins. In most soccer competitions, outside of knockout stages, teams are granted three points for a win and one point for a draw.
- **DRAWS:** If neither team scores or both teams score the same number of goals, the match ends in a draw.
- **EXTRA TIME:** In tournaments or exhibition games, if the match ends in a draw, teams may play extra time—two halves of fifteen minutes each—to find a winner.
- **PENALTY SHOOT-OUTS:** If teams are still tied after extra time, they sometimes go into a penalty shoot-out, where players take turns kicking the ball from the penalty spot. The team with the most goals wins. In the World Cup knockout rounds, games tied after extra time are settled by a shoot-out.

Who Does What?

Soccer sounds simple, right? But although the main rules of the sport are easy to follow, the game can be rather complicated, especially when different formations are used. With eleven players on each team, each player carries out a specific role. Let's learn what these roles can be.

Goalkeeper

The goalkeeper, often referred to as the goalie, is the only player allowed to use their hands, but only in the penalty box, a big rectangle near the goal. While their main job is to defend the net, many goalkeepers do much more. Some, known as sweeper-keepers, step out of their area to pass the ball, defend, and even start attacks. Some goalkeepers include Lev Yashin, Hope Solo, and Manuel Neuer.

DEFENDERS

Defenders focus on protecting the goal by blocking or stopping passes and clearing the ball from their side of the field. They often stay near the goalkeeper to keep the other team away. Communication is important, as a well-disciplined back line works like a synchronized swimming team, perfectly coordinated in marking opponents. Defenders can play in different positions, each important to the team.

QUICK KICKS

According to multiple studies, the average midfielder runs approximately 7 miles (11 km) each match.

Center-backs

These defenders play in the center of the back line, specifically the area in front of the goal. Usually, center-backs are tall or must be able to jump high to head away incoming crosses or score from set pieces. Some teams use center-backs who play as stoppers and sweepers. Some center-backs include Franco Baresi and Sergio Ramos.

Full-backs

These players stay on the left or right side to stop opponents, especially those running along the edges. They also help their team attack by passing the ball or creating scoring chances, making them speedy helpers who can defend and attack! Some examples include Phillip Lahm and Lucy Bronze.

Stoppers

These defenders play slightly ahead of the back line and are aggressive in defense, focusing on stopping the other team's forwards. Some stoppers include Fabio Cannavaro and Virgil van Dijk.

Sweepers

These players are slightly behind the back line and are tasked with "sweeping" up anything that might have gotten past the other defenders. Some incredible sweepers include Franz Beckenbauer and Lothar Matthäus.

Wing-backs

Needing lots of energy to run up and down the field, wing-backs do what full-backs do but also attack. They help their team score and defend. Some players include Cafu and Crystal Dunn.

MIDFIELDERS

Midfielders are the engine room of a team, regularly covering more ground on the pitch than players in other positions, as they play an equal role in defense and offense. They run more than anyone else because they help both in defense and attack. They connect the players at the back with the players up front.

Defensive Midfielders

Positioned in front of the back line to stop attacks and start plays, these players are also known as holding midfielders.

Central Midfielders

Central midfielders control the pace of the game and help both in defense and attack. Often called box-to-box midfielders due to their constant movement across the field.

Attacking Midfielders

These players are positioned behind the forwards. They direct the team's offense and score goals. Known as playmakers, they often wear the iconic number ten jersey.

Wide Midfielders

Wide midfielders play near the sidelines, helping in both defense and attack. They create chances by crossing or passing the ball and often use their strongest foot depending on their side.

FORWARDS

Forwards lead the attack, aiming to score goals while also pressuring goalkeepers and defenders as the first line of defense. Involved in most goals, they create some of soccer's most iconic moments and can play in various positions.

Wingers

Wingers stay on the sides of the field to attack, using speed and dribbling skills. They can be traditional wingers or inverted wingers, depending on their playing style.

Inverted Wingers

These players begin on the sides but move toward the center to take shots or pass to teammates.

Traditional Wingers

Traditional wingers play near the sidelines, running along the edge to pass or cross the ball into the goal area. Called "chalk-on-the-boots" wingers for their closeness to the field lines.

Strikers

Strikers play near the opposing goal in the center, focusing on scoring. These players need accurate kicks and good headers, and they are often called "nines" due to the iconic jersey number they wear.

Center Forwards

Center forwards are positioned in the center, combining scoring and passing roles. Some play as "false nines," staying farther back to help create plays. Center forwards often wear the famous number ten jersey.

The Referees

Matches are overseen by a referee, an official in charge of interpreting and enforcing the Laws of the Game. The referee's duties involve ruling whether something is a foul, calling penalties, disciplining players, keeping track of time, and determining how much stoppage time will be added to each half. Referees are the ultimate authority inside the lines. How they interpret a play can have a great impact on matches.

There are two cards a referee can pull out to show that players have broken the rules: a yellow card and a red card. A yellow card is pulled when a player breaks a rule as a warning and is called a "caution." If a player gets two yellow cards, they get a red card. A red card means a player has to leave the game and cannot be replaced. This card is pulled when a player has broken a serious rule or has displayed bad behavior.

The referee is aided by two assistant referees and a fourth official. Assistant referees, also known as line judges, track whether the ball is out of bounds or if a player is offside. They advise the head referee on certain decisions as needed. The fourth official records the statistics of a game and manages substitutions. Depending on the competition, some matches have video assistant referees, who play a role in video review decisions.

QUICK KICKS

The number ten is a special jersey number that is often worn by a team's most skilled midfielder. This number has been attached to famous players like Messi, Pelé, and Maradona.

What Makes a Legend?

So, what exactly makes a player a soccer legend? The truth is that there isn't one simple answer, but there are many things that can make players extraordinary.

Some players, like Pelé and Lionel Messi, have won so many trophies that their careers are in a league of their own. Others, like Lev Yashin and Franz Beckenbauer, changed how their positions are played, bringing new ideas to the game.

Players like Mia Hamm and George Weah broke barriers, opening doors for others who faced similar challenges. And then there are players like Roberto Baggio and Dennis Bergkamp, who are remembered for their amazing skills and unforgettable plays that wowed fans. Their special moments on the field are unlikely to be repeated.

But what do all these players have in common? They made a huge impact on soccer and inspired generations of young players to follow their dreams. Some even inspired future legends themselves—there may be no bigger compliment than that.

Mini Quiz: Future Stars

Let's test your knowledge on these rising soccer stars!

1. Which country was one of the founder members of FIFA?

- **A.** Brazil
- **B.** Spain
- **C.** England

2. What player can touch the ball with their hands?

- **A.** Striker
- **B.** Central midfielder
- **C.** Goalkeeper

3. How many yellow cards does a player get before they get a red card?

- **A.** Two
- **B.** Three
- **C.** Five

Answer Key: B., C., A.

Everton
Chang
TH24
24

Chapter 2

Goalkeepers

The Last Line of Defense

Playing as a goalkeeper can be a thankless task—they can save ten shots but be remembered for one mistake that costs their team the game, while a forward might miss ten shots but become a hero by scoring one winning goal. Goalkeepers have to be the best in their position to earn a starting spot, as there's only one per team.

They must stay alert, ready to spring into action at any moment, even during a quiet game. Over time, their duties have evolved, but their ability to perform in crucial moments—like stopping a penalty kick—defines greatness. These moments can turn goalkeepers into legends, etching their names into soccer history. Some of these legends helped shape how goalkeeping is played today. Let's take a look at some of the pioneers, stars, and icons who changed the game.

QUICK KICKS

How big are soccer goals?

According to the IFAB's Laws of the Game, adult size goals must be 24 feet (7 m) wide and 8 feet (2 m) high. The goalposts (vertical) and the crossbar (horizontal) must be the same width, which cannot exceed 5 inches (12 cm). Soccer goals typically have white nets to stand out in the field.

Tim Howard, former Everton goalkeeper

Pioneers

The first goalkeepers of the game helped show those who followed how the position should be played. And while many goalkeepers made names for themselves, there was one who changed the game and is still looked up to today: Lev Yashin.

Lev Yashin: The Black Spider

POSITION(S) Goalkeeper
TEAM(S) AND YEARS **Soviet Top League:** Dynamo Moscow (1950–1970)

Once upon a time, goalkeepers stayed in front of the goal, happy just stopping shots and passing the ball. Then came Lev Yashin, nicknamed "The Black Spider" for stopping so many shots it seemed as if he had eight arms. His all-black uniform and occasional flat hat also made him appear like a spider in front of a white net.

Yashin changed the way goalkeeping was played by coming off his line to stop incoming crosses and beat attackers to the ball. He was also known for giving instructions to his back line to help organize them.

Born in Moscow, Russia, in 1929, Yashin debuted as a player in 1950 and played for Dynamo Moscow until 1970. He won five national leagues and three Soviet Cups. He helped the Soviet Union win the 1956 Olympic gold and the 1960 European Championship, and became the first goalkeeper to ever win a Ballon d'Or in 1963.

Yashin made history with his amazing skills and changed the game of soccer forever.

What's the Word?

Pitch

Pitch is another word for the soccer field, so when someone says "pitch," they are referring to the field.

Kicking Facts About Ballon d'Or

- The Ballon d'Or means "Golden Ball" in French, and the trophy is shaped like a shiny golden soccer ball!
- This award was originally meant to honor the best European player within European leagues, but in 1995 the rules changed to include non-European players as well.
- The first Ballon d'Or was first given out in 1956 to honor Stanley Matthews, an English soccer player.
- Lionel Messi holds the record for the most Ballon d'Or wins, with an incredible eight trophies! His rivalry with Cristian Ronaldo (who holds five Ballon d'Or wins) turned this award into a yearly showdown that captivated fans for over ten years.
- In 2018, the Ballon d'Or Féminin was introduced to honor the best woman soccer player in the world. The first winner of the award was Ada Hegerberg from Norway. Since then stars like Alexia Putellas and Aitana Bonmatí have gone on to win the award.
- Ronaldo Nazário de Lima is currently the youngest player to have won a Ballon d'Or at twenty-one years old.

The Golden Zone

At the World Cup, most players want to win the big trophy for their team, but there are also special awards that the best players in the tournament can win. Below are a few of the awards that honor and celebrate individual players and their amazing skills on the field.

- **GOLDEN BALL:** This award is given to the best player in the tournament. The second-best player is sometimes given a Silver Ball, and the third-best player a Bronze Ball. The first Golden Ball was given in 1982 to the Italian Paolo Rossi. Lionel Messi is the only player to have won the Golden Ball twice (2014, 2022).

- **GOLDEN BOOT:** This award is given to the highest scorer in the tournament. It was originally called The Golden Shoe before it was renamed in 2010. If players are tied for goals, then the winner is decided by assists, then by minutes played. No player has ever won this award more than once. Some players that have recently won this award include Kylian Mbappé (2022), Harry Kane (2018), James Rodríguez (2014), Thomas Müller (2010), and Miroslav Klose (2006).

- **GOLDEN GLOVE:** This award is given to the best goalkeeper in the tournament. The Golden Glove was first introduced in 1994 and was originally named the Lev Yashin Award, in honor of the legendary goalkeeper. Some of the goalies that have recently won this award include Emiliano Martínez (2022), Thibaut Courtois (2018), Manuel Neuer (2014), Iker Casillas (2010), and Gianluigi Buffon (2006).

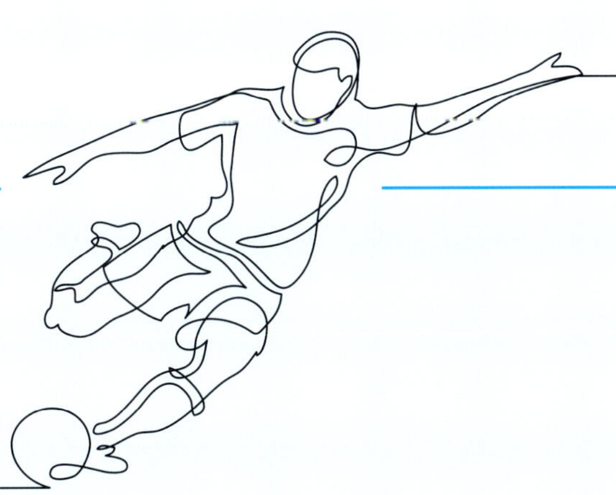

master

Golden Age Stars

During soccer's golden age, goalkeepers were incredibly important players, standing out for their skill and determination. As the "last line of defense," they used speed, courage, and sharp reflexes to protect their teams and stop opponents from scoring. They played a crucial role in their teams' success and earned recognition for their impressive performances.

José Luis Chilavert: The Bulldog

POSITION(S) Goalkeeper

TEAM(S) AND YEARS **Paraguayan Primera División:** Sportivo Luqueño (1982–1984), Club Guaraní (1984–1985)
Argentine Primera División: San Lorenzo (1985–1988), Vélez Sarsfield (1991–2000, 2003–2004)
LaLiga (Spain): Real Zaragoza (1988–1991)
Ligue 1 and Ligue 2 (France): RC Strasbourg (2000–2002)
Uruguayan Primera División: Peñarol (2002–2003)

José Luis Chilavert wasn't just an amazing goalkeeper—he could score goals too! He spent most of his career with a team in Argentina called Vélez Sarsfield, where he played from 1991 to 2000. Over ten seasons, he scored a massive amount of goals, including three goals in one game, called a hat trick, in 1999—a rare thing for goalkeepers! He was named the World's Best Goalkeeper three times (1995, 1997, 1998) and helped Vélez Sarsfield win lots of trophies, including the Copa Libertadores, a huge tournament in South America. For Paraguay's national team, Chilavert played in two World Cups and helped his team reach the second round both times. By the time he retired, Chilavert had scored sixty-seven goals as a goalkeeper.

QUICK KICKS

Rogério Ceni holds the Guinness World Record for the most goals scored by a goalkeeper. Ceni scored 131 goals in his career, placing him among São Paulo FC's top ten goal scorers.

Oliver Kahn: The Titan

POSITION(S) Goalkeeper

TEAM(S) AND YEARS **Bundesliga (Germany):** Karlsruher SC (1987–1994)
Bayern Munich (1994–2008)

Forwards who faced Oliver Kahn barely had time to react before he rushed toward them at full speed to nab the ball. Because of this ferocity, he became known as "The Titan." Kahn began his career with Karlsruher SC of Germany's first division, before playing for German powerhouse Bayern Munich. He was named the best European goalkeeper four years in a row, from 1999 to 2002. Kahn was so dominant that he took home the Golden Ball award—the first and only goalkeeper to earn that honor at a World Cup.

Dino Zoff: The Monument

POSITION(S) Goalkeeper

TEAM(S) AND YEARS **Serie A (Italy):** Udinese (1961–1963), Mantova (1963–1967), Napoli (1967–1972), Juventus (1972–1983)

For most players, winning a European Championship is the biggest achievement of their career, but for Dino Zoff, it was only the start. Between 1972 and 1983, he won six league titles, two domestic cups, and a UEFA Cup with Juventus, establishing himself as not just one of the greatest goalkeepers of his generation, but also one of the greatest Italian players of all time. Zoff was the oldest player to win a World Cup, as well as the only Italian player to win a European Championship and a World Cup. He earned his nickname "The Monument" for having a commanding and calm demeanor on the field.

QUICK KICKS

Since 1992, FIFA's rule states that goalkeepers can't pick up a ball deliberately kicked back by a teammate. They must use their feet, head, or chest. However, if the ball is passed back using a teammate's head or chest, goalkeepers can use their hands.

Modern Icons

Today's goalkeepers are more dynamic than ever, often stepping outside their penalty area to act as an extra defender and initiate plays. With their versatility and leadership, modern goalkeeping icons continue to push the boundaries of what it means to protect the goal and influence the game.

Gianluigi Buffon: Superman

POSITION(S)	Goalkeeper
TEAM(S) AND YEARS	**Serie A (Italy):** Parma (1995–2001), Juventus (2001–2018, 2019–2021) **Serie B (Italy):** Juventus (2006–2007), Parma (2021–2023) **Ligue 1 (France):** Paris Saint-Germain (2018–2019)

Gianluigi Buffon didn't start as a goalkeeper. He started as a midfielder but switched to goalkeeping after watching Thomas N'Kono's heroic saves in the 1990 World Cup. At seventeen, he played his first big game and didn't let in a single goal! This started his legendary twenty-eight-year career. He was nicknamed "Superman" because he was so good at stopping goals. Buffon won 21 trophies with Juventus and even set records like going 974 minutes without letting in a goal. He helped Italy win the 2006 World Cup and earned the best goalkeeper award of the tournament. Buffon retired in 2023 with unmatched achievements in Serie A and international soccer.

What's the Word?

Save

A save is when a goalkeeper stops a ball that could have gone into the goal.

Iker Casillas: Saint Iker

POSITION Goalkeeper

TEAMS AND YEARS **LaLiga (Spain):** Real Madrid (1999–2015)
Liga Portugal (Portugal): Porto (2015–2020)

Iker Casillas is one of the most famous goalkeepers in soccer history. At just nineteen years old, he became the youngest goalkeeper to start and win a Champions League final—and he kept the opposing team from scoring—a feat called a clean sheet! His amazing saves made him a fan favorite from the start. While playing for Real Madrid, Casillas won five league titles, three Champions Leagues, and even a World Cup with Spain. He was so good at making saves that people called him "Saint Iker" because it seemed like he could perform miracles on the field. From 2008 to 2012, he was named the world's best goalkeeper and was honored every year by top soccer organizations.

Tim Howard: The Secretary of Defense

POSITION(S) Goalkeeper

TEAM(S) AND YEARS **Major League Soccer (US):** North Jersey Imperials (1997), MetroStars (1998–2003), Colorado Rapids (2016–2019)
Premier League (England): Manchester United (2003–2006), Everton (2006– 2016)
USL Championship (US): Memphis 901 (2020)

Tim Howard played seven years in the United States before joining Manchester United in 2003, winning three trophies. From 2006 to 2016, he starred for Everton, with 414 games and over one hundred clean sheets. For the US, he won two Gold Cups and set a World Cup record with sixteen saves in 2014. Howard inspired many by sharing his experience with Tourette's syndrome, proving that determination can overcome challenges. He remains a soccer legend and role model!

Keylor Navas: The Panther

POSITION(S) Goalkeeper

TEAM(S) AND YEARS **Costa Rican Primera División:** Saprissa (2005–2010)
Segunda División (Spain): Albacete (2010–2011)
LaLiga (Spain): Levante (2011–2014), Real Madrid (2014–2019)
Ligue 1 (France): Paris Saint-Germain (2019–2023)
Premier League (England): Nottingham Forest (2023, loan)
Argentine Primera División: Newell's Old Boys (2025)
Liga MX (Mexico): Pumas UNAM (2025–Present)

Before Keylor Navas, no soccer player from Costa Rica had ever won the Champions League. In just five seasons with Real Madrid, he won it three times—more than any other male player from North and Central America (Concacaf). Navas earned his nickname "The Panther" for his agility and quick movements on the field. With Costa Rica's national team, Navas helped his country reach the 2014 World Cup quarterfinals, their best performance ever. He also earned big awards, like Concacaf Player of the Year (2014, 2017) and Concacaf Goalkeeper of the Year (2016 to 2018).

Manuel Neuer: The Sweeper Keeper

POSITION(S) Goalkeeper

TEAM(S) AND YEARS **German Regional Leagues:** Schalke 04 II (2004–2006)
Bundesliga (Germany): Schalke 04 (2005–2011), Bayern Munich (2011–Present)

Manuel Neuer became the ultimate example of a "sweeper keeper" in modern times, helping to make this tactic popular. His ability to pass the ball after stopping a shot or breaking up an attack allowed his teams to counterattack quickly.

Neuer began his career at Schalke (2005 to 2011) before joining Bayern Munich in 2011, where he achieved incredible success, including two Champions League titles, twelve league trophies, and a rare "sextuple" in 2020.

He is the only goalkeeper to win two club trebles. During the 2014 World Cup, Neuer completed 242 passes, including many outside the box, and kept four clean sheets, helping Germany win their fourth World Cup while earning the Golden Glove for best goalkeeper. Today, his revolutionary style has become common thanks to his influence.

QUICK KICKS

In 2021, Welsh goalkeeper Tom King scored a goal for Newport County during a game against Cheltenham Town. It was an amazing shot from 105 yards away—that's almost the entire field! This incredible goal not only tied the game for Newport but also set a Guinness World Record for the longest goal ever scored in a competitive match. What a powerful kick!

Hope Solo: The Leaping Lady

POSITION(S) Goalkeeper

TEAM(S) AND YEARS **Women's United Soccer Association:** Philadelphia Charge (2003)
Swedish League: Kopparbergs/Göteborg (2004–2005)
French League: Olympique Lyonnais (2004–2005)
Women's Professional Soccer: Saint Louis Athletica, Atlanta Beat, Boca Raton magicJack (2009–2011)
National Women's Soccer League: Seattle Reign (2013–2016)

Between 2005 and 2016, Hope Solo was the standout goalkeeper for the US Women's National Team, leaping across the goal to stop shots that seemed impossible to save. Holding the starting position for a decade, she set goalkeeping records for the most wins (153), clean sheets (102), matches without losing (55), starts (190), and appearances (202). During her sixteen-year career, Solo helped the United States win the 2015 Women's World Cup, the 2006 and 2014 Concacaf Women's Championship, and two Olympic gold medals (2008 and 2012). At the 2011 World Cup, she earned the Golden Glove, and her performance in 2015 was even better—540 minutes without conceding a goal, five shutouts, and only three goals allowed in seven games, leading to another Golden Glove.

Mini Quiz: Goalies

Think you've got what it takes between the posts? Test your goalkeeper knowledge and keep a clean sheet!

1. What award was originally named after Lev Yashin?

A. Golden Glove
B. Golden Boot
C. Golden Ball

2. What is Dino Zoff's nickname on the field?

A. The Panther
B. The Monument
C. The Sweeper Keeper

3. When can a goalie use their hands to pick up a ball?

A. If the ball is passed back using a teammate's head or chest.
B. If the ball is kicked back by a teammate.
C. If the ball is passed back using a teammate's hands.

Answer Key: A., B., A.

16
16
16
adidas

Chapter 3

Defenders

The Stronghold

Defenders aren't just players who kick the ball away from their goal anymore—they've become important all over the field, even helping to score goals! However, one thing that hasn't changed is how often they serve as the leaders of their teams. Defenders often set the tone for the rest of the team. When a back line is defending well, the rest of the team feels more at ease because they know the defenders can be counted on. As you read about the defenders in this section, you'll notice that nearly all of them wore the captain's armband for the teams they are most closely associated with. This is not a coincidence because defenders are trusted and respected by their teammates!

QUICK KICKS

Do you know why some players wear an armband during matches? The armband signifies that they are the captains of their respective teams. Typically, the armband will also say "Captain" on it, or feature a large letter "C." So when you hear that someone is wearing the captain's armband, it means they are their team's captain.

Crystal Dunn defends the ball against Colombia's Leicy Santos.

Pioneers

Early defenders may be thought of as having limited skills, but some became so good at defending that it forced forwards into upping their game, helping improve the overall quality of play. These players gained the respect of their peers, not just because of their ability, but also because of their leadership skills, which inspired their teammates to reach great heights.

Bobby Moore: The Gentleman

POSITION(S) Center-back

TEAM(S) AND YEARS **Football League First Division (England):** West Ham United (1958–1974)
Football League Second Division (England): Fulham (1974–1977)
North American Soccer League (US): San Antonio Thunder (1976, loan), Seattle Sounders (1978)
2. Division (Denmark): Herning Fremad (1978)
American Soccer League (US): Carolina Lightnin' (1983)

Bobby Moore was seventeen years old when he made his first professional appearance. He made over six hundred appearances for West Ham from 1958 to 1974, helping them win two domestic trophies. At just twenty-two, he was named the team captain for England. A few years later, he led England to the final of the 1966 World Cup at home, providing an assist on the final goal as his team defeated West Germany 4-2. Minutes later, he became the first and only English captain to win and raise the World Cup.

What's the Word?

Loan

A loan is when a player plays temporarily for a certain team they are not contracted to play for.

Franz Beckenbauer: The Kaiser

POSITION(S) Center-back

TEAM(S) AND YEARS **Bundesliga (Germany):** Bayern Munich (1964–1977), Hamburger SV (1980–1982)
North American Soccer League (US): New York Cosmos (1977–1980, 1983)

When Franz Beckenbauer began playing for Bayern Munich in 1964, no one knew his best position. He played as a forward, midfielder, and defender before solving the puzzle himself—by creating a new role: the sweeper. As a center-back, he stopped attackers, distributed the ball, and joined the attack when needed. As captain, he led Munich to consecutive European Cups, four league titles, and four domestic cups between 1968 and 1976. He also made 103 appearances for West Germany, captaining the team to victory in the 1974 World Cup and the 1972 European Championship.

Golden Age Stars

During the golden age of soccer, roughly from the mid-1970s to the early 2000s, some players turned defending into an art form just as matches began to be broadcast worldwide. Global audiences were suddenly exposed to these defenders on a regular basis, and they soon became the gold standard, with young players seeking to emulate them on the field. During the late 1980s and 1990s, Italy's Serie A became the home for some of the best defenders in the world.

Franco Baresi: The Lombardy Hero

POSITION(S)	Center-back
TEAM(S) AND YEARS	**Serie A (Italy):** Milan (1977–1997)

Franco Baresi played for Milan his entire career, serving as captain for fifteen years. He was a tough but intelligent defender who won seventeen club trophies, including three European Cups. He was a starter for his team at the 1990 and 1994 World Cups, helping Italy finish third and second, respectively. In all, he made eighty-one appearances for Italy. When Baresi retired, Milan retired his shirt number (six) to honor him.

Cafu (Marcos Evangelista de Morais): The Pendolino

POSITION(S) Full-back, Wing-back

TEAM(S) AND YEARS **Campeonato Brasileiro Série A:** São Paulo (1989–1995), Juventude (1995), Palmeiras (1995–1997)
LaLiga (Spain): Real Zaragoza (1995)
Serie A (Italy): Roma (1997–2003), Milan (2003–2008)

As a former midfielder, Cafu earned the nickname of "*Pendolino*," an Italian high-speed train, because of his ability to recover the ball and initiate attacks. Cafu collected ten trophies in his first five seasons as a professional. In Italy, he won six trophies, including a Champions League. Internationally, he won two World Cups (1994, 2002) and two Copa América titles (1997, 1999). He also earned 142 caps with Brazil, more than any other player. Cafu is the only male player in history to play in three World Cup finals, having done so in 1994, 1998, and 2002.

Fierce Rivalries

Soccer is full of exciting matchups that make fans jump out of their seats! Whether it's two famous teams battling for the win or star players going head-to-head, these clashes bring tons of unforgettable moments. They can even unite or divide entire cities. Let's check out some of the coolest rivalries in the game!

EL CLÁSICO

REAL MADRID VS. BARCELONA (SPAIN)

This is Spain's biggest soccer showdown! Two of the most famous teams in the world face off, and fans everywhere tune in to watch. Superstars like Messi and Ronaldo played in this match.

SUPERCLÁSICO

BOCA JUNIORS VS. RIVER PLATE (ARGENTINA)

In Argentina, this game is a huge deal! The stadiums are packed, the fans are loud, and the energy is off the charts.

OLD FIRM DERBY

CELTIC VS. RANGERS (SCOTLAND)

Dating back over one hundred years, when these two Scottish teams play, it feels like a championship match every time. The fans are super passionate, and the games are always full of surprises.

GOAT Showdowns

LIONEL MESSI vs. CRISTIANO RONALDO

The ultimate GOAT debate. These two legends have battled for Ballon d'Ors, Champions League glory, and fan loyalty for over ten years.

ROY KEANE vs. PATRICK VIEIRA

Midfield warriors from Manchester United and Arsenal. Their fiery clashes defined Premier League intensity in the early 2000s.

MIA HAMM vs. BIRGIT PRINZ

These two women dominated soccer in the early 2000s and were often compared as the best in the world.

Paolo Maldini: Il Capitano

POSITION(S) Full-back, Center-back
TEAM(S) AND YEARS **Serie A (Italy):** Milan (1984–2009)

As the son of Milan legend Cesare Maldini, Paolo Maldini debuted with the club at sixteen years old. In the twenty-five years that he played soccer, he won nineteen trophies, including five Champions League titles. Maldini captained Milan and the Italian national team, for which he made 126 appearances, earning the nickname "*Il Capitano*" (The Captain). He played in four World Cups (1990, 1994, 1998, and 2002), finishing in third place in 1990 and second place in 1994. He also finished as a runner-up in the 2000 Euro. Maldini retired in 2009 as Milan's all-time leader in appearances (902). The club retired his jersey number (three), stipulating that it could only be used by one of his children, a fitting tribute to Milan's favorite son.

Daniel Passarella: The Great Captain

POSITION(S) Center-back
TEAM(S) AND YEARS **Primera División C (Argentina):** Sarmiento (1971–1973)
Primera División (Argentina): River Plate (1973–1982, 1988–1989)
Serie A (Italy): Fiorentina (1982–1986), Inter Milan (1986–1988)

Daniel Passarella was known for his leadership skills and rose to prominence at River Plate. There, he won seven league titles and scored ninety goals, before playing for Italian sides Fiorentina and Inter Milan. Passarella was named Argentina's captain in the lead-up to the 1978 World Cup, thriving as he led Argentina to its first World Cup trophy. He was also a member of the 1986 World Cup-winning squad. In all, Passarella made seventy appearances for Argentina, scoring twenty-two goals.

Gaetano Scirea: The Elegant Defender

POSITION(S) Center-back

TEAM(S) AND YEARS **Serie A (Italy):** Atalanta (1972–1974), Juventus (1974–1988)

Gaetano Scirea had a more measured approach to defending than most center-backs of his time and stood out because of his elegance on the ball and his ability to read the game. He made over five hundred appearances for Juventus, winning fourteen trophies, including a European Cup. Throughout his career, he managed to win every UEFA club and domestic title available at the time. A fixture on Italy's squad, Scirea earned seventy-eight caps and was a 1982 World Cup winner.

Lilian Thuram: The Giant of Guadeloupe

POSITION(S) Center-back, Full-back

TEAM(S) AND YEARS **Division 1 (France):** Monaco (1991–1996)
Serie A (Italy): Parma (1996–2001), Juventus (2001–2006)
LaLiga (Spain): Barcelona (2006–2008)

Whether playing as a center-back or a full-back, Lilian Thuram was a rock on defense. He spent much of his club career in Italy, winning six trophies. Thuram also made 142 appearances for France, playing in three World Cups and three Euros. During the 1998 France World Cup, Thuram led France's back line as the nation won its first World Cup while conceding only two goals. He also helped France win Euro 2000. Thuram scored both of his career international goals in one game—helping France beat Croatia 2-1 in the semifinals of the 1998 World Cup.

What's the Word?

Cap

Caps are how many times a player has played for their official team in international matches. For instance, if you play for the US team, anytime you play a big game against another country, you earn a cap.

Modern Icons

In the modern era, defenders have taken on more offensive duties, with some defenders being crucial to their team's offense. But while taking on new duties, they've had to do so without neglecting actual defending. Several of the players in this section were members of clubs that won multiple titles because, as the saying goes, defense wins championships.

Lucy Bronze: Boss It Like Bronze

POSITION(S) Full-back

TEAM(S) AND YEARS **FA Women's Premier League Northern Division (England):** Sunderland (2007–2010)
Women's Super League (England): Everton (2010–2012), Liverpool (2012–2014), Manchester City (2014–2017, 2020–2022), Chelsea (2024–Present)
Division 1 Féminine (France): Lyon (2017–2020)
Liga F (Spain): Barcelona (2022–2024)

Lucy Bronze is one of England's most amazing soccer players! She's won five Champions League trophies—more than any other English player—and twenty-one domestic titles. She helped her teams, Lyon and Barcelona, win the treble (that means three major trophies in one season) not just once, but three times!

In 2020, she was voted the best women's soccer player in the world by FIFA—the first English player ever to win that award. Lucy has played over 130 times for England, helping her country win the European Championship twice (2022, 2025). She was also a star at the 2019 World Cup, earning the Silver Ball for being one of the top players.

England in Play

1. England held the first ever international soccer match in 1872 against Scotland, which ended in a draw.
2. Wembley Stadium in England, is known as the "Home of Football." The original stadium was opened in 1923 and demolished in 2003. A new Wembley Stadium was built in 2007.
3. England is the location for the famous 1923 FA Cup final, which became known as the "White Horse Final" because it was so overcrowded that it took one policeman and his white horse to clear the field.

Fabio Cannavaro: The Berlin Wall

POSITION(S) Center-back

TEAM(S) AND YEARS **Serie A (Italy):** Napoli (1991–1995), Parma (1995–2002), Inter Milan (2002–2004), Juventus (2004–2006, 2009–2010)
LaLiga (Spain): Real Madrid (2006–2009)
UAE Pro League (United Arab Emirates): Al Ahli Dubai (2010–2011)

Even though Italy has always had lots of amazing defenders to choose from, Fabio Cannavaro stood out. He wasn't very tall like some of the others, but he was super fast and worked really hard. That helped him become one of the best players in Italy's top league, called Serie A. Over his club career, he won nine major trophies! Cannavaro also made 136 appearances for Italy, with his best moment coming in the 2006 Germany World Cup. His performance was so dominant that it earned him the nickname "The Wall of Berlin" and the Silver Ball. That same year, he also won the Ballon d'Or and the FIFA Player of the Year award, becoming the first defender to win the player of the year award.

Crystal Dunn: The Mighty Mouse

POSITION(S) Wing-back, Midfielder, Striker

TEAM(S) AND YEARS **National Women's Soccer League (US):** Washington Spirit (2014–2016), North Carolina Courage (2018–2020), Portland Thorns FC (2020–2023), NJ/NY Gotham FC (2024)
FA Women's Super League (England): Chelsea FC Women (2017–2018)
Première Ligue (France): Paris Saint-Germain (2025–Present)

Crystal Dunn is a soccer superstar who's played for top teams in the United States, England, and France! She is known to her fans as "The Mighty Mouse" for her fierce and speedy play on the field. She won the National Women's Soccer League (NWSL) MVP and Golden Boot in 2015 for scoring the most goals in the league. She helped her teams win multiple NWSL Championships and Shields, and she played a big role in winning the 2019 World Cup and a gold medal at the 2024 Olympics with Team USA. She has made over 160 appearances for the US Women's National Team and scored twenty-five goals, showing she's one of the most talented and hardworking players in the game.

Philipp Lahm: The Master of Adaptability

POSITION(S) Full-back, Defensive midfielder

TEAM(S) AND YEARS **Regionalliga Süd (Germany):** Bayern Munich II (2001–2003), **Bundesliga (Germany):** Bayern Munich (2002–2017), VfB Stuttgart (2003–2005, loan)

When Philipp Lahm was a young soccer player, he joined a team on loan and was supposed to be a backup right-back. But instead of waiting around, he started playing on the left side and did so well that he became one of the main starters! Upon returning to Bayern Munich in 2005, Lahm continued to play in whatever position the club needed him to play and was eventually named captain. He went on to win twenty-one trophies with Munich, including a treble in 2013. Lahm also earned 113 caps for Germany, playing every minute of the 2006, 2010, and 2014 World Cups. In 2014, Lahm played as both a defensive midfielder and right-back as he captained Germany to its fourth World Cup, proving that adaptability pays off.

Rafael Márquez: The Michoacán Kaiser

POSITION(S) Center-back

TEAM(S) AND YEARS **Liga MX (Mexico):** Atlas (1996–1999, 2016–2018), León (2012–2014)
Ligue 1 (France): Monaco (1999 to 2003)
LaLiga (Spain): Barcelona (2003–2010)
Major League Soccer (US): New York Red Bulls (2010–2012)
Serie A (Italy): Hellas Verona (2014–2015)

During his twenty-year career, Rafael Márquez won some of the sport's highest honors alongside some of the greatest players of his era. During his time at Barcelona, Márquez won twelve trophies, including the famous sextuple of 2009. He had similar success with Mexico, earning 147 caps. Márquez's highlights include winning the 1999 Confederations Cup—making Mexico the only Concacaf nation to win the tournament—and two Gold Cups (2003, 2011). He holds the distinction of being one of five male players to play in five World Cups.

Carles Puyol: Lionheart

POSITION(S) Center-back, Full-back

TEAM(S) AND YEARS **LaLiga (Spain):** Barcelona (1999–2014)

Whenever Carles Puyol finished a match, there was no doubt he had left every ounce of himself on the field. As club captain, Puyol held others to the same high standard. Much like his hero, Paolo Maldini, Puyol was equally capable at playing as a full-back or center-back. He came through the Barcelona academy, making 662 appearances for the club. During his fifteen-year career with the club, he won twenty-one trophies, including the famous sextuple of 2009. Puyol was a key member of Spain's national team, earning one hundred caps and winning the 2010 World Cup and Euro 2008. During the 2010 World Cup semifinal match against Germany, he scored the game-winning goal in the 72nd minute, sealing Spain's spot in the final.

Sergio Ramos: The Gambler

POSITION(S) Center-back, Full-back

TEAM(S) AND YEARS **Segunda División B (Spain):** Sevilla Atlético (2003–2004)
LaLiga (Spain): Sevilla (2004–2005, 2023–2024), Real Madrid (2005–2021)
Ligue 1 (France): Paris-Saint Germain (2021–2023)
Liga MX (Mexico): Monterrey (2025–Present)

Sergio Ramos defends with the ferocity of an attacker and always seems to go big or go home. It's how he has scored over one hundred goals . . . and received thirty red cards. Ramos made 671 appearances for Madrid, all while winning twenty-two trophies, including four Champions League trophies. He scored seventy-two times for Real Madrid, including in two Champions League finals (2014, 2016). Ramos was a constant presence in the Spanish national team during their most successful era. In all, he has made 180 appearances for Spain, more than any other player, while winning the 2010 World Cup and two Euros (2008, 2012).

Virgil van Dijk: The Stopper

POSITION(S) Center-back

TEAM(S) AND YEARS **Eredivisie (Netherlands):** Groningen (2011–2013)
Scottish Premiership: Celtic (2013–2015)
Premier League (England): Southampton (2015–2018), Liverpool (2018–Present)

Every so often, a player comes along whose ability to defend one-on-one puts him in a category of his own. Virgil van Dijk is that type of player. How good is he? During the 2018–2019 Premier League season, no player dribbled past him. Van Dijk has been key to Liverpool's success over the past decade, winning nine trophies, including a Champions League. Although van Dijk has not had the same success at the international level, he may yet be able to win trophies with the Netherlands.

QUICK KICKS

The fastest goal in World Cup history was scored just 2.8 seconds after kick-off! It was scored by Hakan Şükür of Turkey in 2002, against South Korea.

Mini Quiz: Defending the Field

Let's see how much you know about these trusted and respected players!

1. What is the primary role of defenders in soccer?

- **A.** To assist the goalkeeper in taking goal kicks
- **B.** To score goals for their team
- **C.** To protect the goal by blocking or stopping passes

2. Which type of defender is known for staying on the left or right side of the field?

- **A.** Sweepers
- **B.** Stoppers
- **C.** Full-backs

3. Which player won a gold medal at the 2024 Olympics with Team USA?

- **A.** Crystal Dunn
- **B.** Rafael Márquez
- **C.** Lucy Bronze

Answer Key: C., C., A.

Joma
unicef

Chapter 4

Midfielders

The Heart of the Team

Soccer's constant evolution has meant that present-day players have more responsibilities than in the past. This isn't new to midfielders, who have always had to perform defensive and offensive duties, given their position on the pitch. Whether it's dictating the game's tempo through quick, short passes or running back to help the defenders, midfielders are tasked with making a team tick. Because the midfield is often packed with players, midfielders must repeatedly maneuver around other players, developing precise control over the ball. Some midfielders are so good at finding space that they often unlock defenses with a single pass, while others provide a goal threat of their own.

QUICK KICKS

Because they are in the middle of the field, midfielders can see the whole field and help their team plan when to attack, defend, or slow down. They are often quick thinkers that can change the game with just one clever pass.

Xavi Hernandéz of Barcelona dribbles the ball away from Lolo of Sevilla during their Copa del Rey Last 16 match in 2010.

Pioneers

The midfielders who established themselves as pioneers were players whose abilities were ahead of their time. Besides being great players, these pioneers were key members of teams that thrilled fans—either by winning big or by playing in exciting ways.

Bobby Charlton: Sir Bobby

POSITION(S) Attacking midfielder

TEAM(S) AND YEARS **Football League First Division (England):** Manchester United (1956–1973)
Football League Third Division (England): Preston North End (1974–1975)
League of Ireland: Waterford United (1976)
National Soccer League (Australia): Newcastle KB United (1978), Blacktown City (1980)
National Premier Leagues Western Australia: Perth Azzurri (1980)

Bobby Charlton played for Manchester United for seventeen years, winning a European Cup and seven domestic titles. A playmaker capable of scoring with either foot, he is second in all-time goals (249) and appearances (758) for Manchester United. Charlton made 106 appearances and scored forty-nine goals for England. His crowning moment came in the 1966 World Cup, where he started every match and scored three goals, helping England win the trophy. A Ballon d'Or winner (1966), Charlton never received a red card throughout his career—a testament to his spirit of fair play.

What's the Word?

Total Football

Total football is a style of play that focuses on the idea that any player can play in any position on the field at any given time. It is a style popularized by both Ajax and the Netherlands national teams.

Johan Cruyff: The Oracle

POSITION(S) Attacking midfielder

TEAM(S) AND YEARS **Eredivisie (Netherlands):** Ajax (1964–1973, 1981–1983), Feyenoord (1983–1984)
LaLiga (Spain): Barcelona (1973–1978)
North American Soccer League (US): Los Angeles Aztecs (1979), Washington Diplomats (1980–1981)
Segunda División (Spain): Levante (1981, loan)

Johan Cruyff was so smooth on the ball that his slim figure often appeared to be floating over the pitch as he dribbled past opponents to score. Cruyff was the clear leader of the Ajax team that won three European Cups in a row. He also led the Netherlands to the World Cup final in 1974 while earning the tournament's Golden Ball. His influence in the game is unparalleled. As a player in the 1970s, he represented the Dutch school of total football that captured the public's imagination. As a coach in the 1990s, he led Barcelona to a European Cup and eight domestic titles in what has been dubbed "The Dream Team."

Johan Neeskens: The Dutch Lung

POSITION(S) Central midfielder

TEAM(S) AND YEARS **Eerste Divisie (Netherlands):** RCH (1968–1970)
Eredivisie (Netherlands): Ajax (1970–1974), Groningen (1984–1985)
LaLiga (Spain): Barcelona (1974–1979)
North American Soccer League (US): New York Cosmos (1979–1984)
United Soccer League (US): South Florida Sun (1985)
Major Indoor Soccer League (US): Kansas City Comets (1985–1986)
2. Liga (Switzerland): Baar (1987–1990), Zug (1990–1991)

Johan Neeskens's ability to run without tiring earned him the nickname of the "Dutch Lung." While he stood out because of his defensive capabilities, Neeskens also scored goals, tallying four goals in the 1974 World Cup and winning the Silver Boot. A part of the Ajax team that won three consecutive European Cups, Neeskens also appeared in back-to-back World Cup finals with the Netherlands in 1974 and 1978.

Netherlands' Soccer Legacy

As one of the founders of FIFA, it is no surprise that the Netherlands has made its mark on the sport of soccer, from exciting tournaments to favorite traditions that fans know and love. Although the Netherlands' national team is one of the best and has made it to the World Cup three times (1974, 1978, and 2010), they have yet to win a World Cup. They won their first major trophy in 1988—the UEFA European Championship. During major soccer tournaments, the country turns orange in support of their team who is nicknamed "*Oranje.*" The Dutch's team badge is a lion, which is the national animal of the Netherlands.

Golden Age Stars

By the golden age of soccer, midfielders were adding new facets to their game, with some of them providing as much of a goal threat as strikers. But beyond their abilities as players, it was their intangibles—leadership, influence, the ability to step up—that truly set them apart. As you read, take notice of how many midfielders stepped up when it mattered most for their respective teams.

Roberto Baggio: The Divine Ponytail

POSITION(S) Attacking midfielder

TEAM(S) AND YEARS **Serie C1 (Italy):** Vicenza (1982–1985)
Serie A (Italy): Fiorentina (1985–1990), Juventus (1990–1995), Milan (1995–1997), Bologna (1997–1998), Inter Milan (1998–2000), Brescia (2000–2004)

Roberto Baggio was one of the most brilliant players soccer has seen. Known as "The Divine Ponytail" because of his cool hairstyle, Baggio was one of the top scorers in Serie A and one of the best goal makers, always helping his teammates score with smart passes and free kicks. Following the 1992–1993 season, he was named the Ballon d'Or and FIFA World Player of the Year winner. Baggio helped Italy finish third at the 1990 World Cup and scored five goals at the 1994 tournament to lead Italy to the final. In all, Baggio earned fifty-six caps for Italy, scoring twenty-seven goals.

David Beckham: Becks

POSITION(S) Wide midfielder, Central midfielder

TEAM(S) AND YEARS
Premier League (England): Manchester United (1992–2003)
Football League Third Division (England): Preston North End (1995, loan)
LaLiga (Spain): Real Madrid (2003–2007)
Major League Soccer (US): Los Angeles Galaxy (2007–2012)
Serie A (Italy): Milan (2009, 2010, loan)
Ligue 1 (France): Paris Saint-Germain (2013)

David Beckham was one of the most accurate crossers of the ball the world has seen. A product of the Manchester United academy, he played for the club for over ten years and even won the treble during the 1998–1999 season, including providing the game-winning assist in the Champions League final. Beckham made 115 appearances for England, representing his nation at three World Cups. He was so good at kicking the ball from free kicks that people still say they want to "bend it like Beckham" when they try to curve the ball just like he did.

Luis Figo: Lusitanian Lightning

POSITION(S) Winger, Wide midfielder, Attacking midfielder

TEAM(S) AND YEARS **Primeira Divisão (Portugal):** Sporting CP (1989–1995)
LaLiga (Spain): Barcelona (1995–2000), Real Madrid (2000–2005)
Serie A (Italy): Inter Milan (2005–2009)

With his lightning speed, silky footwork, and accurate crosses, Luis Figo was the type of player who made any team better. During his twenty-year career, Figo won twenty-one trophies, including a Champions League. He won the Ballon d'Or in 2000 and the 2001 FIFA Player of the Year award. Figo represented Portugal in two World Cups and three Euros, including a runner-up finish at the 2004 Euro. He scored 32 goals in his 127 appearances, the second-most appearances for Portugal.

Ruud Gullit: Master of All Trades

POSITION(S) Attacking midfielder, Central midfielder, Center forward

TEAM(S) AND YEARS **Eredivisie (Netherlands):** HFC Haarlem (1979–1982), Feyenoord (1982–1985), PSV (1985–1987)
Serie A (Italy): Milan (1987–1994), Sampdoria (1993–1994, loan; 1994–1995)
Premier League (England): Chelsea (1995–1998)

Ruud Gullit was a jack of all trades and a master of all. The embodiment of total football, he could play as a midfielder, forward, or defender while excelling at those positions. During his time at Milan, Gullit won ten trophies, including two European Cups. He also collected a Ballon d'Or (1987). Gullit earned sixty-six caps for the Netherlands. At Euro 1988, he made history with the Dutch, scoring in the final of Euro 1988 to defeat the Soviet Union and lift his nation's first major international trophy.

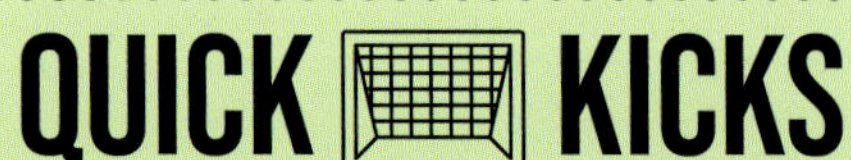

Matthäus is one of five players to play at five World Cups. He played in the 1982, 1986, 1990, 1994, and 1998 tournaments.

Michael Laudrup: The Prince of Denmark

POSITION(S) Attacking midfielder

TEAM(S) AND YEARS
1. Division (Denmark): KB (1981), Brøndby (1982–1983)
Serie A (Italy): Lazio (1983–1985), Juventus (1985–1989)
LaLiga (Spain): Barcelona (1989–1994), Real Madrid (1994–1996)
J1 League (Japan): Vissel Kobe (1996–1997)
Eredivisie (Netherlands): Ajax (1997–1998)

Michael Laudrup had a way of making everything look effortless. Whether dribbling past defenders to score from a tight angle or assisting teammates with a lob of the ball, Laudrup had creativity that knew no bounds. He signed with Barcelona in 1989, helping "The Dream Team" win a European Cup and seven domestic titles. Laudrup was also a standout with Denmark, for whom he made 105 appearances and scored thirty-seven goals.

Lothar Matthäus: The Tank

POSITION(S) Defensive midfielder, Attacking midfielder, Center-back

TEAM(S) AND YEARS
Landesliga Bayern-Mitte (Germany): Herzogenaurach (1978–1979, 2018)
Bundesliga (Germany): Borussia Mönchengladbach (1979–1984), Bayern Munich (1984–1988, 1992–2000)
Serie A (Italy): Inter Milan (1988–1992)
Major League Soccer (US): MetroStars (2000)

Nicknamed "*Der Panzer*" (the Tank) because of how opponents would bounce off him as he made his way down the field like a tank, Lothar Matthäus played as a midfielder for most of his career before switching to sweeper in his later years. He is most closely associated with Bayern Munich, with whom he won thirteen trophies. Matthäus is the most capped German player of all time with 150 appearances. He made his debut at the Euro 1980, in which West Germany won. Matthäus's finest moment came during the 1990 World Cup when he led West Germany to its third title, defeating Diego Maradona's Argentina in the final, a rematch of the 1986 final.

Diego Maradona: El Diez

POSITION(S) Attacking midfielder

TEAM(S) AND YEARS **Primera División (Argentina):** Argentinos Juniors (1976–1981), Boca Juniors (1981–1982, 1995–1997), Newell's Old Boys (1993–1994)
LaLiga (Spain): Barcelona (1982–1984), Sevilla (1992–1993)
Serie A (Italy): Napoli (1984–1991)

Diego Maradona made his professional debut at the age of fifteen for Argentinos Juniors. With his dazzling dribbling, passing, and ability to take over a game by himself, Maradona came to define what an Argentine *Diez* (ten) should be. He became synonymous with Napoli, leading the club to win five trophies during his seven seasons there, despite only having two titles before his arrival.

Maradona earned ninety-one caps and scored thirty-four goals for Argentina. He played in four World Cups, but the 1986 tournament was his defining moment, as he made ten goal contributions, leading Argentina to a second world title. In 2000, he was named the FIFA Player of the Century, alongside Pelé. There is a reason that no Argentine player has ever been as beloved as Maradona.

QUICK KICKS

Diego Maradona scored both goals in Argentina's 2–1 victory over England in the 1986 World Cup quarterfinals. In the 55th minute, Maradona dribbled past four players and the goalkeeper to score the game-winning goal, which fans voted Goal of the Century in a 2002 FIFA poll.

Michel Platini: Le Roi

POSITION(S) Attacking midfielder, Central midfielder

TEAM(S) AND YEARS **Division 1 (France):** Nancy (1972–1979), Saint-Étienne (1979–1982)
Serie A (Italy): Juventus (1982–1987)

Nicknamed "*Le Roi*" (The King), Michel Platini was a playmaker who often outscored strikers. Between 1982 and 1985, Platini helped Juventus win five titles, including a European Cup, even finishing as Serie A top scorer three times. He made seventy-two appearances and scored forty-one goals for France. During Euro 1984, held in France, Platini scored nine goals in five matches to help France win its first international trophy. He was named player of the tournament and finished as top scorer. He won three consecutive Ballon d'Or awards (1983, 1984, 1985).

Carlos Valderrama: El Pibe

POSITION(S) Attacking midfielder, Central midfielder

TEAM(S) AND YEARS **Categoría Primera A (Colombia):** Unión Magdalena (1980–1984), Millonarios (1984), Deportivo Cali (1985–1987, 1996–1997, loan), Independiente Medellín (1992–1993), Atlético Junior (1993–1995)
Division 1 (France): Montpellier (1987–1991)
LaLiga (Spain): Real Valladolid (1991–1992)
Major League Soccer (US): Tampa Bay Mutiny (1995–1997, 1999–2001), Miami Fusion (1997–1999), Colorado Rapids (2001–2002)

Sporting a blonde-dyed long curly mane, and a black mustache, Carlos Valderrama was hard to miss. Known as *El Pibe* (The Boy), Valderrama served as a creative linchpin. He made 111 appearances for Colombia, scoring eleven goals and playing in three World Cups. He helped Colombia to a third-place finish at the 1987 Copa América, earning the Golden Ball. Although he was not a prolific goal scorer, Valderrama was great at creating chances for his teammates to score. His twenty-six assists in a single Major League Soccer regular season is a league record that still stands.

Zico (Arthur Antunes Coimbra): The Little Rooster

POSITION(S) Attacking midfielder

TEAM(S) AND YEARS **Campeonato Brasileiro Série A:** Flamengo (1971–1983, 1985–1989)
Serie A (Italy): Udinese (1983–1985)
J.League (Japan): Kashima Antlers (1991–1994)

Zico was an attacking midfielder whose ability to dribble, assist, and score with flair earned him the nickname "*O Galinho*" (Little Rooster). Zico helped establish Flamengo as a South American powerhouse team as he led them to twelve titles, including a Copa Libertadores trophy. Zico is Flamengo's all-time leader in goals (508) and appearances (731). Despite a career plagued with injuries, Zico made seventy-one appearances for Brazil, recording forty-eight goals and twenty-one assists. He played in three World Cups, helping Brazil finish third in 1978.

Zinedine Zidane: The Artist

POSITION(S) Attacking midfielder

TEAM(S) AND YEARS **Division 1 (France):** Cannes (1988–1992), Bordeaux (1992–1996)
Serie A (Italy): Juventus (1996–2001)
LaLiga (Spain): Real Madrid (2001–2006)

Whenever Zinedine Zidane dribbled the ball on the field, it was like watching an artist at work. He won fourteen club trophies during his career, including one Champions League. If Zidane was an artist, his favorite canvas was the international stage, where he made 108 appearances and scored thirty-one goals for France. In 1998, Zidane led France to its first World Cup trophy, scoring two goals in the final and winning the Ballon d'Or that year. Zidane also won Euro 2000 with France and was named player of the tournament. In 2006, he spearheaded France's run to the World Cup final, winning the tournament's Golden Ball. Sometimes, it's hard to pick an artist's best masterpiece.

Modern Icons

These days, teams stick closer together when they defend, making it super hard for the other side to move the ball. So midfielders have to be really smart and sneaky to find space and make cool plays in those crowded areas. Because of this, you will often see midfielders scan the field looking for options, as they look for open players to whom they can deliver passes. Many of the names you will see next are among the most creative midfielders out there.

Aitana Bonmatí: The Golden Girl

POSITION(S)	Central midfielder
TEAM(S) AND YEARS	**Liga F (Spain):** Barcelona (2016–Present)

Growing up, Aitana Bonmatí had limited options available when it came to youth soccer teams, so she joined a boys' club. There she stood out enough to be signed by Barcelona, her current team. Bonmatí has already won twenty-four trophies at the club level, including a treble (2020–2021) and a quadruple (2023–2024). She helped Spain win the 2023 Women's World Cup, making five goal contributions and claiming the Golden Ball. In 2024, she won the UEFA Nations League. Bonmatí recently won three Ballon d'Or Féminin awards and the FIFA Women's Player of the Year award (2023, 2024).

Kevin De Bruyne: The Assist King

POSITION(S) Attacking midfielder

TEAM(S) AND YEARS
Belgian Pro League: Genk (2008–2012)
Premier League (England): Chelsea (2012–2014), Manchester City (2015–2025)
Bundesliga (Germany): Werder Bremen (2012–2013, loan), VfL Wolfsburg (2014–2015)
Serie A (Italy): Napoli (2025–Present)

Kevin De Bruyne is so adept at understanding space and setting up goals that he has established himself as one of the best playmakers of his generation. Since joining Manchester City in 2015, De Bruyne has played a large role in the club's success, winning sixteen trophies, including the 2022-2023 treble. Over that span, he has made over four hundred appearances, registering 174 assists and over one hundred goals. De Bruyne has also earned 115 caps for Belgium, playing in three World Cups and three Euros. During the 2018 World Cup, he scored one goal and provided two assists to help Belgium secure third place.

Steven Gerrard: Red Heart

POSITION(S) Central midfielder

TEAM(S) AND YEARS **Premier League (England):** Liverpool (1998–2015)
Major League Soccer (US): Los Angeles Galaxy (2015–2016)

With his leadership, versatility, and never-give-up attitude, Steven Gerrard represented everything a captain should be. A lethal striker from long distance, he scored 120 goals in league action—only second to Frank Lampard in the Premier League era. Gerrard spent twelve years as Liverpool captain, winning eight trophies, including a Champions League. He earned 114 caps with England from 2000 to 2014, scoring twenty-one goals. During the 2005 Champions League final, while trailing Milan 3-0, Gerrard scored a goal in the second half and rallied his teammates to level the score. Liverpool went on to win on penalty kicks. Gerrard may not have won the Premier League, but he won the hearts of all Liverpool fans.

Xavi Hernandéz: The Conductor

POSITION(S) Central midfielder

TEAM(S) AND YEARS **Segunda División B (Spain):** Barcelona B (1997–2000)
LaLiga (Spain): Barcelona (1998–2015)
Qatar Stars League: Al Sadd (2015–2019)

If Barcelona and Spain played to the tune of tiki-taka, Xavi Hernandéz's constant movement and passing dictated the tempo. Hernandéz's habit of scanning around the field before and after receiving the ball always put him one step ahead of everyone else. A product of the Barcelona academy, he won twenty-five trophies with the club, including a sextuple (2008-2009) and a treble (2014-2015). He was also a key member of the Spanish side that won the World Cup (2010) and two Euros (2008, 2012). His performance at the Euro 2008 earned him the player of the tournament award. Hernandéz finished his international career with eighty-two caps and twenty goals for Spain.

What's the Word?

Sextuple

A sextuple also referred to as sextuplet is when a team wins six major trophies in one season or calendar year—this is a rare achievement in soccer!

Andrés Iniesta: The Illusionist

POSITION(S) Central midfielder

TEAM(S) AND YEARS **Segunda División B (Spain):** Barcelona B (2000–2003)
LaLiga (Spain): Barcelona (2002–2018)
J1 League (Japan): Vissel Kobe (2018–2023)
UAE Pro League (UAE): Emirates Club (2023–2024)

Andrés Iniesta dribbled past opponents with such ease that it looked like he was making the ball disappear from one foot and reappear on the other. Smart on the ball, Iniesta would selflessly pass up scoring opportunities to instead assist his teammates. He came through the Barcelona academy and won thirty trophies, including a sextuple (2008-2009) and a treble (2014-2015). Iniesta scored the game-winning goal in the 2010 World Cup final, helping Spain win its first World Cup. He also won two Euro titles (2008, 2012) and was named player of the tournament at Euro 2012. He made 131 appearances for Spain.

Toni Kroos: The Waiter

POSITION(S) Central midfielder, Defensive midfielder

TEAM(S) AND YEARS **3. Liga (Germany):** Bayern Munich II (2007–2008)
Bundesliga (Germany): Bayern Munich (2007–2014), Bayer Leverkusen (2009–2010, loan)
LaLiga (Spain): Real Madrid (2014–2024)

Toni Kroos was not as athletic as some midfielders, but his intelligence more than made up for it. Able to cut through offensive lines by playing his trademark low-driven passes, Kroos was known as "The Waiter" because he would serve the ball on a silver platter to his teammates. Kroos's career was largely spent with Bayern Munich and Real Madrid. At Munich, he won ten trophies, including a treble during the 2012-2013 season. From 2014 to 2024, Kroos won twenty-three trophies with Madrid, including five Champions League titles. He made 114 appearances for Germany and won the 2014 World Cup, playing every minute of the tournament and making six goal contributions.

More Than a Game

On March 11, 2011, Japan was hit with a devastating earthquake and tsunami that wreaked havoc throughout the nation. As the country recovered from the devastation, Japan's women's national team headed to Germany to participate in the World Cup.

The Japanese team wanted to make their country proud, and they made it all the way to the final match against the United States. Even though they were losing 2–1 in extra time and had never beaten the US before, Japan scored a super late goal in the 117th minute! That tied the game and sent it into a penalty shoot-out, which Japan won.

Their triumph reminded people that even in dark times unity, resilience, and determination can lead to something great. The team's story inspired many athletes and sparked more interest in women's soccer in Asia.

Did You Know . . .

- Before every match Japanese players would hold up a banner that said "Thank You" to the world for their support after the earthquake.
- Japan had never beaten the US in twenty-five matches, making their World Cup win one for the history books.
- Homare Sawa was the player who scored the equalizer at the 117th minute to tie the World Cup final with the US.
- There were over thirteen million people watching the 2011 World Cup in the US alone—it was the most-watched match in cable television history.

Global Awareness

After the tsunami in Japan, countless people around the world sent help, from sending food to sending hopeful messages. This is why Japanese players held up a sign in gratitude after each game. Many people from all over the world cheered for Japan. Their World Cup journey reminded people that sports can bring people together during hard times. But adults aren't the only ones that can make a difference; kids can make a difference too. Whether its writing a kind note, learning about another culture, or helping someone near you, small actions make big impacts.

QUESTIONS TO CONSIDER

- What is one small kind thing you can do this week?
- What are some ways that sports can teach people about unity and teamwork?
- What does it mean to be part of team, especially during tough times?

Frank Lampard: Super Frank

POSITION(S) Central midfielder

TEAM(S) AND YEARS **Premier League (England):** West Ham United (1995–2001), Chelsea (2001–2014), Manchester City (2014–2015)
Football League Second Division (England): Swansea City (1995–1996, loan)
Major League Soccer (US): New York City FC (2015–2016)

Frank Lampard scored 177 goals in league play—more than any other midfielder in the Premier League era. He was able to score regularly without neglecting his playmaking or defensive duties, a testament to his discipline. He is best known for his time at Chelsea, where he won thirteen titles, including one Champions League. He also made 106 appearances and scored twenty-nine goals for England.. He is among the most revered players in Chelsea history.

Carli Lloyd: Unstoppable

POSITION(S) Attacking midfielder, Center forward

TEAM(S) AND YEARS **W-League (US):** Central Jersey Splash (1999), New Brunswick Power (2000), South Jersey Banshees (2001), New Jersey Wildcats (2004)
Women's Professional Soccer (US): Chicago Red Stars (2009), Sky Blue (2010), Atlanta Beat (2011)
National Women's Soccer League (US): Western New York Flash (2013–2014), Houston Dash (2015–2017), NJ/NY Gotham FC (2018–2021)
FA WSL Spring Series (England): Manchester City (2017, loan)

When Carli Lloyd was on her game, no one could stop her. Lloyd was a staple of the US national team, with whom she won two Women's World Cups (2015, 2019) and two Olympic Gold medals (2008, 2012). During the 2015 World Cup, she scored six goals in the last four matches, including a hat trick in the final. Lloyd's performance earned her the tournament's Golden Ball and Silver Boot, and that year's Ballon D'Or. She also won the FIFA Women's Player of the Year award in 2016. By the time Lloyd retired in 2021, she was second in all-time appearances (316), third in all-time goals (134), and sixth in all-time assists for the US.

Luka Modrić: The Cruyff of the Balkans

POSITION(S) Central midfielder

TEAM(S) AND YEARS **Prva HNL (Croatia):** Dinamo Zagreb (2003–2008), Inter Zaprešić (2004–2005, loan)
Bosnian Premier League: Zrinjski Mostar (2003–2004, loan)
Premier League (England): Tottenham Hotspur (2008–2012)
LaLiga (Spain): Real Madrid (2012–2025)
Serie A (Italy): Milan (2025–Present)

As a child growing up during wartime, Luka Modrić had slim prospects of becoming a professional soccer player. But Modrić made the most of his opportunities, eventually joining Real Madrid, where he won twenty-eight trophies—including an astounding six Champions Leagues! A stalwart for Croatia, he has played in four World Cups and led Croatia to a second-place finish in 2018. He won the Ballon d'Or in 2018.

Pavel Nedvěd: The Czech Fury

POSITION(S) Wide midfielder, Attacking midfielder

TEAM(S) AND YEARS **Czech First League (Czech Republic):** Škoda Plzeň (1990–1992), Dukla Prague (1990–1992, loan), Sparta Prague (1992–1996)
Serie A (Italy): Lazio (1996–2001), Juventus (2001–2009)

A player with a powerful shot, high work rate, and the ability to kick with both feet, Pavel Nedvěd was Europe's best-kept secret for a while. After spending the first seven years of his career playing for Czech clubs, Nedvěd burst onto the global soccer scene during Euro 1996 and never looked back. In 2001, Juventus signed him to replace Zinedine Zidane, and he helped them win four domestic titles in two years, while winning the 2003 Ballon d'Or. Nedvěd made ninety-one appearances for the Czech Republic, playing in the 2006 World Cup and three Euros. Notably, he helped his nation reach the Euro 1996 final, Czechia's best finish at the tournament.

Alexia Putellas: The Catalan Queen

POSITION(S) Central midfielder, Winger

TEAM(S) AND YEARS **Liga F (Spain):** Espanyol (2008–2011), Levante (2011–2012), Barcelona (2012–Present)

Alexia Putellas grew up idolizing Barcelona soccer players like Andrés Iniesta and Ronaldinho, modeling her game after them. She combines technical skill and intelligence on the field. Today, she is a member of Barcelona and has won twenty-two trophies, a treble (2020–2021), and a quadruple (2023–2024). Alexia Putellas has scored more than 209 goals—more than any other woman who's played for Barcelona! She helped Spain win the 2023 Women's World Cup and captained the squad as it won the 2023–2024 UEFA Nations League. She is a two-time Ballon d'Or Féminin and two-time FIFA Women's Player of the Year (2021, 2022).

Megan Rapinoe: The Outspoken

POSITION(S) Attacking midfielder, Winger

TEAM(S) AND YEARS **Women's Professional Soccer (US):** Chicago Red Stars (2009–2010), Philadelphia Independence (2011), Boca Raton MagicJack (2011)
W-League (Australia): Sydney (2011)
USL W-League (US): Seattle Sounders (2012)
Division 1 Féminine (France): Lyon (2013–2014)
National Women's Soccer League (US): OL Reign (2013–2023)

Whether gliding past tackles or taking on off-the-field issues, Megan Rapinoe always held her ground. A two-time Women's World Cup winner (2015, 2019) and an Olympic gold medalist (2012), she earned 203 caps for the United States, registering sixty-three goals and seventy-three assists. During the 2019 World Cup, Rapinoe made nine goal contributions, including scoring in the final to help the Americans win the trophy. Her individual awards that year included winning the Golden Ball and Golden Boot at the tournament, as well as the Ballon d'Or and the Best FIFA Women's Player award. Rapinoe was known for valiantly using her platform to speak about social justice issues.

Ronaldinho (Ronaldo de Assis Moreira): The Smile of Soccer

POSITION(S) Attacking midfielder, Winger

TEAM(S) AND YEARS **Campeonato Brasileiro Série A (Brazil):** Grêmio (1998–2001), Flamengo (2011–2012), Atlético Mineiro (2012–2014), Fluminense (2015)
Ligue 1 (France): Paris Saint-Germain (2001–2003)
LaLiga (Spain): Barcelona (2003–2008)
Serie A (Italy): Milan (2008–2011)
Liga MX (Mexico): Querétaro (2014–2015)

Few players have had as much fun on the field or brought joy to so many as Ronaldinho. A born entertainer who could make the ball do whatever he wanted, he always smiled when he was on the field. He played for some of the biggest clubs in the world, winning eleven trophies, including the Champions League and Copa Libertadores. Ronaldinho made ninety-seven appearances for Brazil, helping the team win the World Cup (2002), Copa América (1999), and Confederations Cup (2005). A Ballon d'Or (2005) winner and two-time FIFA World Player of the Year recipient, Ronaldinho inspired a generation of players to play *jogo bonito*.

JOGO BONITO: A BRAZILIAN ART FORM

Jogo bonito—a term attributed to World Cup winners Pelé and Didi—is Portuguese for "beautiful game," and it is both a description as well as a philosophy directly tied to Brazil's soccer identity. The use of flair and creativity in the form of flicks, tricks, and other eye-catching foot skills are all examples of *jogo bonito*. Over the years, players like Pelé, Ronaldinho, and Neymar have become some of the best examples of this style. Their individual creativity displays the ingenuity found in *jogo bonito*:

- Ronaldinho's *elástico*
- Neymar's stepovers
- Pelé lobbing the ball over opponents

Next time you're on the field, why not try to play *jogo bonito*?

10
15

Homare Sawa: A National Treasure

POSITION(S) Attacking midfielder

TEAM(S) AND YEARS **Nadeshiko League (Japan):** Yomiuri Beleza (1991–1999, 2004–2008, 2009, loan; 2010), INAC Kobe Leonessa (2011–2015)
USL W-League (US): Denver Diamonds (1999–2000)
Women's United Soccer Association (US): Atlanta Beat (2001–2003)
Women's Professional Soccer (US): Washington Freedom (2009–2010)

Homare Sawa was a prodigy, making her professional debut at the age of twelve. She won twenty-one domestic titles in Japan and one International Women's Club Championship. In 2011, Sawa captained Japan to its first World Cup trophy, scoring five goals to claim both the Golden Ball and the Golden Boot. Following her performance, she became the first Asian player to win FIFA World Player of the Year (2011). In all, Sawa earned 205 caps and scored eighty-three goals for Japan, helping Japan win an AFC Women's Asian Cup (2014), a gold medal at the Asian Games (2010), and a silver medal at the Olympics (2012).

Yaya Touré: The Ivorian Buffalo

POSITION(S) Defensive midfielder, Central midfielder

TEAM(S) AND YEARS
Belgian First Division (Belgium): Beveren (2001–2003)
Vyshcha Liha (Ukraine): Metalurh Donetsk (2003–2005)
Super League Greece 1: Olympiacos (2005–2006, 2018)
Ligue 1 (France): Monaco (2006–2007)
LaLiga (Spain): Barcelona (2007–2010)
Premier League (England): Manchester City (2010–2018)
Chinese Super League: Qingdao Huanghai (2019)

Seeing Yaya Touré go on a run from midfield at full speed was as awe-inspiring as it was intimidating. A physically imposing specimen, Touré could stop an attack, initiate a counterattack, and score in one play. Touré was most successful at Barcelona and Manchester City, winning a sextuple with Barcelona and eight domestic trophies with Manchester City. He made 101 appearances for Ivory Coast, playing in three World Cups and six African Cup of Nations tournaments. He was the captain for the Ivory Coast side that won the 2015 African Cup of Nations.

Goooaaal!

We've arrived at the heart of a soccer team—the midfielders. These players are super important to the flow of the game, deciding when to slow things down to maintain possession and when to speed up to launch attacks. Time to show off your soccer IQ like a midfield maestro!

1. Which type of midfielder often wears the number ten jersey?
   A. Defensive Midfielder
   B. Wide Midfielder
   C. Attacking Midfielder

2. Which type of midfielder plays near the sidelines and helps create chances by crossing the ball?
   A. Central Midfielder
   B. Wide Midfielder
   C. Defensive Midfielder

3. What nickname is often given to midfielders because they control the pace and link defense with attack?
   A. The Runners
   B. The Brain or the Heart
   C. The Attackers

4. Which midfielder never received a red card during their entire career in soccer?
   A. Bobby Charlton
   B. David Beckham
   C. Luka Modrić

5. Who was awarded the FIFA Player of the Century in the year 2000?
   A. Frank Lampard
   B. Toni Kroos
   C. Diego Maradona

6. Who won two Ballon d'Or Féminin awards and two FIFA Women's Player of the Year awards?
   - A. Aitana Bonmatí
   - B. Homare Sawa
   - C. Carli Lloyd

7. Which player was playing for the US team against Japan in the 2011 World Cup?
   - A. Alexia Putellas
   - B. Megan Rapinoe
   - C. Carli Lloyd

8. What player was known for playing in the tiki-taka style?
   - A. Yaya Touré
   - B. Xavi Hernández
   - C. Carlos Valderrama

9. Which style of play is considered a Brazilian art form?
   - A. *Jogo bonito*
   - B. Tiki-taka
   - C. Total football

10. Which player helped Spain win its first World Cup?
    - A. Aitana Bonmatí
    - B. Xavi Hernández
    - C. Andrés Iniesta

Answer Key: C., B., B., A., C., A., B., B., A., C.

USA
13
14

Chapter 5

Forwards

The Goal Machines

Let's be honest: Most soccer players start off wanting to be forwards. After all, forwards score goals, and goals win games, right? But scoring goals can be difficult, so players find different ways to do it, relying on their unique attributes to make the position their own. Some use their speed, others rely on their sense of space, and some even provide more goal assists than they score! There are, of course, some who know how to do a little bit of everything and put it all together in one beautiful goalscoring package. The players in this section are record-setters and record-breakers whose highlight reels include some of the most exciting moments the sport has ever known.

QUICK KICKS

The highest-scoring soccer game ever ended with a score of 149–0! It happened in Madagascar in 2002 when the losing team kept scoring their own goals in protest.

Alex Morgan of the US and Nathalie Björn of Sweden playing under pressure at the FIFA Women's World Cup 2023.

Pioneers

Pioneer forwards were notorious not only for scoring goals, but also because they gave everyone who came after them something to aspire to. Some of these players set records that are still being chased today. As you read, try to keep track of what some of these records are.

Michelle Akers: The First Lady of American Soccer

POSITION(S)	Center forward, Central midfielder
TEAM(S) AND YEARS	**Damallsvenskan (Sweden):** Tyresö FF (1990, 1992, 1994)

Michelle Akers was a huge part of the US women's team and helped make it one of the best in the world. Her strength, skill, and leadership inspired tons of players who came after her. She scored the first goal in team history and netted both goals in the inaugural Women's World Cup (1991) final, as the United States defeated Norway 2–1. She also claimed Golden Boot and Silver Ball honors. By the time Akers retired, she had helped the US win a second World Cup (1999) and an Olympic gold medal (1996). She earned 155 caps, registering 107 goals and thirty-seven assists for the United States.

Alfredo Di Stéfano: The Blond Arrow

POSITION(S) Center forward

TEAM(S) AND YEARS **Argentine Primera División:** River Plate (1945–1949), Huracán (1945–1946, loan)
Campeonato Profesional (Colombia): Millonarios (1949–1953)
LaLiga (Spain): Real Madrid (1953–1964), Espanyol (1964–1966)

Known as the "Blond Arrow" due to his hair color, speed, and accuracy in front of a goal, Alfredo Di Stéfano became a legend at Real Madrid, where he won five European Cups and nine domestic titles. Di Stéfano scored 308 goals in 396 appearances for Madrid. He finished as LaLiga's top scorer five times. Born in Argentina, he played for Argentina, Colombia, and Spain, winning the 1947 Copa América with his native country. A two-time Ballon d'Or winner (1957, 1959), Di Stéfano holds the distinction of winning the Super Ballon d'Or in 1989—the only such trophy to be awarded.

What's the Word?

Treble

A treble is when a team wins three major trophies in a single season, and just like a sextuple, it is a rare and impressive achievement in the world of soccer.

Stanley Matthews: The Wizard of Dribble

POSITION(S) Winger

TEAM(S) AND YEARS **Football League First Division (England):**
Stoke City (1932–1947, 1961–1965), Blackpool (1947–1961)
Eastern Canada Professional Soccer League:
Toronto City (1961, 1965, loans)

Stanley Matthews's discipline and dedication to fitness enabled him to continue playing until he was fifty, making him the oldest player to feature in England's top division. A master dribbler, he inspired a generation of English boys to play the game. Matthews played from 1932 to 1965, winning a domestic cup with Blackpool. He earned fifty-four caps with England, scoring eleven goals, and played in two World Cups. He holds the distinct honor of being the only soccer player to be knighted while still active (1965).

The Most Iconic Hat Tricks

- England vs. West Germany (1966 World Cup Final) - Geoff Hurst's hat trick was the first ever in the men's World Cup final.
- US vs. Japan (2015 Women's World Cup Final) - Carli Lloyd's hat trick holds the record for the only one ever scored in a Women's World Cup final.
- Barcelona vs. Real Madrid (2007 *El Clásico*) - Lionel Messi became the youngest player ever to score a hat trick in *El Clásico*, at just nineteen years old.
- Real Madrid vs. Manchester United (2003 Champions League) - Ronaldo Nazário's hat trick earned him a standing ovation from rival fans and knocked Manchester United out of the tournament.
- Zambia (2020 and 2024 Olympics) - Barbra Banda holds the record for three Olympic hat tricks, the most in women's Olympic soccer history.

Pelé (Edson Arantes do Nascimento): O Rei

POSITION(S) Center forward, Striker

TEAM(S) AND YEARS **Campeonato Brasileiro Série A (Brazil):** Santos (1956–1974)
North American Soccer League (US): New York Cosmos (1975–1977)

Pelé's ability to dribble past players with flair and score eye-catching goals on the world's biggest stages made him one of the most recognized athletes of the twentieth century. He is the youngest player to win a World Cup at just seventeen years old. He won the World Cup's Best Young Player (1958), Silver Ball (1958), and Golden Ball (1970) awards.

The all-time goal-scorer for Santos (643 goals), Pelé helped the Brazilian team become a global powerhouse, leading them to win two Copa Libertadores titles, two Intercontinental Cups, and nineteen domestic titles. Pelé announced himself to the world during the 1958 World Cup and went on to become the only player to win the tournament three times (1958, 1962, 1970). He made ninety-two appearances for Brazil while scoring seventy-seven goals. If you're wondering how valued Pelé was during his playing career, all you need to know is that in 1961 Brazil's president declared him a national treasure. Who are we to argue?

QUICK KICKS

Pelé and Diego Maradona are some of the first names that come to mind when discussing the greatest players of all time. But did you know they never won a Ballon d'Or? The reason for this is that the Ballon d'Or was originally created to honor the best players in Europe, until the rules changed in 1995 to include players from outside Europe who played for European clubs.

Ferenc Puskás: The Booming Cannon

POSITION(S) Striker, Center forward

TEAM(S) AND YEARS **Nemzeti Bajnokság I (Hungary):** Budapest Honvéd (1943–1956)
LaLiga (Spain): Real Madrid (1958–1966)

With a super strong left leg and surprising speed, Ferenc Puskás was a natural at scoring goals. Puskás scored an outstanding eighty-four goals in eighty-five appearances for Hungary, helping the Hungarians reach the final of the 1954 World Cup and winning the Golden Ball at the tournament. During his time with Real Madrid, he won ten trophies, including three consecutive European Cups. In 1960, during the European Cup final against Eintracht Frankfurt, Puskás scored four goals in a 7–3 victory. Puskás was such an amazing goal scorer that in 2009 FIFA established the Puskás Award, given each year to the individual who scored the best goal that season.

Top Five Longest Careers

The average soccer player lasts about eight to eleven years playing the game, but the following list of players have stayed much longer.

- The center-forward Kazuyoshi Miura also known as "King Kazu" has been playing the game for over thirty-nine years. He started in 1986 and is still presently playing for Atletico Suzuka in the Japanese Football League.
- Goalkeeper Peter Shilton played soccer for thirty-one years, starting in 1966 and retiring in 1997. He has the most competitive appearances (1,387 matches).
- The center-forward Roger Milla played the game for thirty-one years and still holds the record for the oldest goal scorer in World Cup history (forty-two years old). He played from 1967 to 1996.
- The Brazilian midfielder Formiga (Miraildes Maciel Mota) played soccer for twenty-six years and holds the Guinness World Record for longest international career in women's soccer. She began playing in 1993 and retired in 2022.
- One of the greatest goalkeepers in the sport, Gianluigi Buffon played for twenty-eight years, finally retiring at the age of forty-five. He played from 1995 to 2023.

Golden Age Stars

The golden age of soccer was filled with strikers who were all vying to be the best. During this era, it was classic center forwards who thrived, bringing a level of physicality that hadn't been seen before.

Gabriel Batistuta: Batigol

POSITION(S) Striker

TEAM(S) AND YEARS **Primera División (Argentina):** Newell's Old Boys (1988–1989), River Plate (1989–1990), Boca Juniors (1990–1991)
Serie A (Italy): Fiorentina (1991–2000), Roma (2000–2003), Inter Milan (2003, loan)
Qatar Stars League (Qatar): Al-Arabi (2003–2005)

Gabriel Batistuta played nine seasons for Fiorentina, leading the club to two domestic trophies. By the time he left Fiorentina, he was their all-time top scorer in Serie A action, with 151 goals. Batistuta earned seventy-eight caps with Argentina, scoring fifty-six goals. He played in three World Cups and three Copa América tournaments, winning the latter tournament twice (1991, 1993). Batistuta also won two Copa América Golden Boots (1991, 1995). He's the only player to score hat tricks at two different World Cups (1994, 1998). Batistuta's impact in Florence can still be felt today, as residents of Florence still smile when his name is mentioned.

Dennis Bergkamp: The Iceman

POSITION(S) Striker, Center forward

TEAM(S) AND YEARS **Eredivisie (Netherlands):** Ajax (1986–1993)
Serie A (Italy): Inter Milan (1993–1995)
Premier League (England): Arsenal (1995–2006)

Dennis Bergkamp's calmness under pressure allowed him to score extraordinary goals and play impossible passes, earning him the nickname "The Iceman." Bergkamp began his career with Ajax, helping the fabled side win five trophies in six seasons, but he became a legend at Arsenal. There, he shone as a second striker, registering 120 goals and ninety-four assists in 423 appearances. He won eleven trophies, one of them by finishing a Premier League season undefeated. Bergkamp was also a standout with the Netherlands, netting thirty-seven goals in seventy-nine appearances. He played in two World Cups and three Euros, scoring in each competition.

George Best: The Fifth Beatle

POSITION(S) Winger

TEAM(S) AND YEARS

Football League First Division (England): Manchester United (1963–1974)

Southern League Division One North (England): Dunstable Town (1974)

Football League Fourth Division (England): Stockport County (1975)

League of Ireland (Ireland): Cork Celtic (1975–1976)

North American Soccer League (US): Los Angeles Aztecs (1976, 1977–1978), Fort Lauderdale Strikers (1978–1979), San Jose Earthquakes (1980–1981)

Football League Second Division (England): Fulham (1976–1977)

Scottish Premier Division (Scotland): Hibernian (1979–1980)

Football League Third Division (England): AFC Bournemouth (1982–1983)

National Soccer League (Australia): Brisbane Lions (1983)

George Best brought a mixture of speed, unpredictability, and high energy. An avid scorer known for his mazy dribbles, long hair, and good looks, Best has since been called the "Fifth Beatle." The winger made 470 appearances and scored 179 goals for Manchester United, helping the club win four domestic titles and the 1968 European Cup while claiming the 1968 Ballon d'Or. He earned thirty-seven caps for Northern Ireland but never played in a World Cup. In the latter part of the twentieth century, a saying began to circulate that described his place in Manchester United lore: "Pelé good, Maradona great, George Best."

Eusebio da Silva Ferreira: The Black Pearl

POSITION(S) Center forward, Striker

TEAM(S) AND YEARS **Moçambola (Mozambique):** Sporting Lourenço Marques (1957–1960)
Primeira Divisão (Portugal): Benfica (1961–1975), Beira-Mar (1976)
North American Soccer League (US): Boston Minutemen (1975), Toronto Metros-Croatia (1975–1976), Las Vegas Quicksilvers (1976–1977)
Mexican Primera División (Mexico): Monterrey (1975)
Segunda Divisão (Portugal): União de Tomar (1977–1978)
American Soccer League (US): New Jersey Americans (1978–1979)
Major Indoor Soccer League (US): Buffalo Stallions (1979–1980)

Eusebio da Silva Ferreira joined SL Benfica as a teenager and became the club's greatest legend. Known for his speed and powerful right shot, he was a nightmare for opposing defenses in his heyday. Eusebio registered 638 goals in 614 matches for Benfica, winning twenty-eight domestic titles and the 1962 European Cup. He also won the 1965 Ballon d'Or and two European Golden Shoes (1968, 1973). Eusebio represented Portugal sixty-four times and scored forty-one goals. He played in the 1966 World Cup, winning the Golden Boot with nine goals and leading Portugal to a third-place finish.

Gerhard "Gerd" Müller: Der Bomber

POSITION(S) Striker

TEAM(S) AND YEARS **Bezirksliga Schwaben-Nord (Germany):** 1861 Nördlingen (1963–1964)
Bundesliga (Germany): Bayern Munich (1964–1979)
North American Soccer League (US): Fort Lauderdale Strikers (1979–1981)

Gerd Müller was lethal inside the penalty area and he spent most of his career with Bayern Munich, helping the club win twelve trophies, including three consecutive European Cups. He is Bayern Munich's all-time top goal scorer, with 566 goals in 607 appearances. He won the 1970 Ballon d'Or and two European Golden Shoes (1970, 1972). Müller's 365 goals in Bundesliga action are still a record. He earned sixty-two caps for West Germany, scoring sixty-eight goals. Müller won the 1972 European Championship and the 1974 World Cup, scoring the winning goal in the World Cup final and earning Golden Boot honors for both tournaments.

Mia Hamm: Wonder Woman

POSITION(S) Forward, Attacking midfielder

TEAM(S) AND YEARS **Women's United Soccer Association (US):** Washington Freedom (2001–2003)

Mia Hamm was fifteen when she made her debut with the US women's national team in 1987, becoming the youngest player to do so. By the turn of the century, she had become the face of US soccer and a global icon. Hamm made 276 appearances and provided 305 goal contributions for the US, more than any other American. She also won two Women's World Cups (1991, 1999), two Olympic gold medals (1996, 2004), and one Olympic silver medal (2000). At the club level, she won a domestic championship with the Washington Freedom in 2003.

Hamm is a two-time FIFA Women's World Player of the Year (2001, 2002) and won the US Soccer Female Player of the Year award five consecutive times between 1994 and 1998. Elegant on the field and eloquent off of it, Hamm is still the standard for all US female players.

QUICK KICKS

Mia Hamm has not just made an impact on the field, but she's also made an impact off the field. She founded the Mia Hamm Foundation, which helps families affected by bone marrow disease and promotes women in sports.

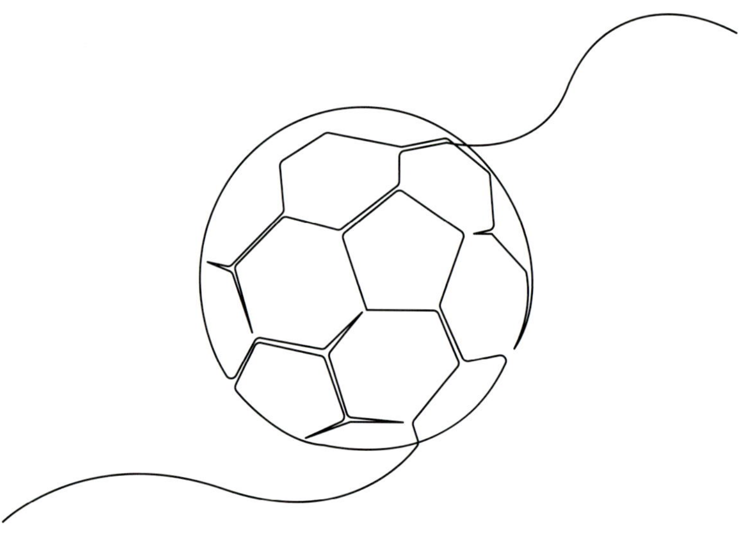

9

Ronaldo Nazário de Lima: The Phenomenon

POSITION(S) Striker, Center forward

TEAM(S) AND YEARS **Campeonato Brasileiro Série A:** Cruzeiro (1993–1994), Corinthians (2009–2011)
Eredivisie (Netherlands): PSV (1994–1996)
LaLiga (Spain): Barcelona (1996–1997), Real Madrid (2002–2007)
Serie A (Italy): Inter Milan (1997–2002), Milan (2007–2008)

A two-time Ballon d'Or winner (1997, 2002) and three-time FIFA Player of the Year (1996, 1997, 2002), Ronaldo Nazário de Lima could dribble through back lines like no one else. With Brazil, he won the 2002 World Cup, two Copa América trophies (1997, 1999), and the 1997 FIFA Confederations Cup. He won the Golden Ball (1998) and the Golden Shoe (2002) at the World Cup. He was the Most Valuable Player (1997) and joint top scorer at Copa América (1999). He earned ninety-eight caps and scored sixty-two goals for Brazil.

Hugo Sánchez: Hugol

POSITION(S) Striker

TEAM(S) AND YEARS **Mexican Primera División:** UNAM (1976–1982), América (1992–1993), Atlante (1994–1995), Atlético Celaya (1997)
North American Soccer League (US): San Diego Sockers (1979–1980, loan)
LaLiga (Spain): Atlético Madrid (1981–1982, loan; 1982–1985), Real Madrid (1985–1992, 1997), Rayo Vallecano (1993–1994)
2. Liga (Austria): Linz (1995–1996)
Major League Soccer (US): Dallas Burn (1996)

Known for his acrobatic style, Hugo Sánchez scored goals everywhere he played. He's best remembered for his time at Real Madrid, where he netted 208 goals in 282 matches and helped them win nine trophies. He was the joint winner of the 1989–1990 European Golden Shoe. Sánchez played fifty-eight times for Mexico, scored twenty-nine goals, and appeared in three World Cups and the 1993 Copa América. He helped Mexico win the 1977 Concacaf Championship and reach the 1993 Copa América final.

Hristo Stoichkov: The Dagger

POSITION(S) Center forward, Winger

TEAM(S) AND YEARS
V Group (Bulgaria): Hebros Harmanli (1982–1983)
A Group (Bulgaria): CSKA Sofia (1984–1990, 1997–1998, loan)
LaLiga (Spain): Barcelona (1990–1995, 1996–1998)
Serie A (Italy): Parma (1995–1996)
Saudi Premier League (Saudi Arabia): Al-Nassr (1998)
J1 League (Japan): Kashiwa Reysol (1998–1999)
Major League Soccer (US): Chicago Fire (2000–2002), D.C. United (2003)

Able to play as center forward or out wide, Hristo Stoichkov often could cut through defenders and score. During his time at Barcelona, he helped the club win fifteen trophies, including its first European Cup. He earned eighty-three caps and scored thirty-seven goals for Bulgaria, playing in two World Cups and the 1996 Euro. At the 1994 World Cup, Stoichkov scored six goals and helped Bulgaria reach the quarterfinals, winning the tournament's Golden Boot and Bronze Ball awards. A 1994 Ballon d'Or winner and 1990 European Golden Shoe joint winner, Stoichkov is the greatest Bulgarian player of all time.

Marco van Basten: The Swan of Utrecht

POSITION(S) Striker, Center forward

TEAM(S) AND YEARS
Eredivisie (Netherlands): Ajax (1981–1987)
Serie A (Italy): Milan (1987–1995)

Few players have looked as good as Marco van Basten while scoring. Van Basten won nineteen trophies throughout his career, including two European Cups at Milan, where he scored 129 goals in 205 matches. He tallied twenty-four goals in fifty-eight appearances for the Netherlands, participating in one World Cup and two Euros. He was the Golden Boot winner at Euro 1988, scoring five goals as the Netherlands claimed its first international trophy. Despite playing his last match at twenty-eight years old because of injuries, van Basten won three Ballon d'Or awards (1988, 1989, 1992), one FIFA World Player of the Year award (1992), and one European Golden Shoe (1985).

George Weah: King George

POSITION(S) Striker, Center forward

TEAM(S) AND YEARS **Liberian Premier League:** Bong Range United (1984–1985), Mighty Barrolle (1985–1986), Invincible Eleven (1986–1987)
Cameroon Premiere Division: Tonnerre Yaoundé (1987–1988)
Division 1 (France): Monaco (1988–1992), Paris Saint-Germain (1992–1995), Marseille (2000–2001)
Serie A (Italy): Milan (1995–2000)
Premier League (England): Chelsea (2000, loan), Manchester City (2000)
UAE Football League: Al Jazira (2001–2003)

Fast, strong, and proficient at playing between the lines, George Weah was the prototype for modern forwards. Weah played for some of the biggest clubs in the world, winning eleven domestic trophies. He made seventy-three appearances for Liberia, scoring eighteen goals. Although Weah never had the chance to play in a World Cup, he helped Liberia qualify for the African Cup of Nations in 1996 and 2002. Weah is the only African player to win the Ballon d'Or and FIFA World Player of the Year award, both of which he won in 1995.

Sun Wen: The Steel Rose

POSITION(S) Striker, Center forward

TEAM(S) AND YEARS **Chinese Women's Premier Football League (China):** Shanghai (1989–2000)
Women's United Soccer Association (US): Atlanta Beat (2001–2002)
Women's Super League (China): Shanghai SVA (2003, 2006)

Sun Wen grew up watching her father play soccer games, which sparked her interest in the game. By the time she was seventeen, Sun had made her debut with China's national team, which she represented at four World Cups. During the 1999 World Cup, she registered seven goals and three assists while helping China reach the finals. The team's only loss in that event came via penalty shoot-out. Her performance earned her the tournament's Golden Ball and a shared Golden Boot. Sun also helped China win five Asian Cups (1991, 1993, 1995, 1997, 2006) and a silver medal at the 1996 Olympics. In all, she earned 152 caps for China, scoring 106 goals.

QUICK KICKS

In 2002, Sun Wen and Michelle Akers were named joint winners for the FIFA Female Player of the Century award.

Modern Icons

Soccer today looks different from how it used to! In the past, the center forward was usually the player who scored the most goals. But now, speedy wingers who play out wide are scoring tons of goals too—sometimes even more than the main strikers! As teams come up with new game plans, the top goal scorers might look totally different in the future.

Neymar da Silva Santos Jr.: The Gem

POSITION(S) Winger, Center forward, Attacking midfielder

TEAM(S) AND YEARS **Campeonato Brasileiro Série A (Brazil):** Santos (2009–2013, 2025–Present)
LaLiga (Spain): Barcelona (2013–2017)
Ligue 1 (France): Paris Saint-Germain (2017–2023)
Saudi Pro League (Saudi Arabia): Al-Hilal (2023–2025)

As a teenager, Neymar da Silva Santos Jr. became the best player in South America with Santos, showing off Brazil's *jogo bonito* style. At twenty-two, he joined Barcelona and won eight trophies, including a treble. Later, he starred for Paris Saint-Germain, winning thirteen more. Neymar played in three World Cups and three Copa América tournaments, helping Brazil reach the 2014 semifinals while winning the Bronze Ball. He also helped Brazil win its first Olympic gold medal in 2016 and the 2013 Confederations Cup. With 128 games and seventy-nine goals, he's Brazil's all-time top scorer.

Samuel Eto'o: The Indomitable Lion

POSITION(S) Striker

TEAM(S) AND YEARS **LaLiga (Spain):** Real Madrid (1997–2000), Espanyol (1999, loan), Mallorca (2000, loan; 2000–2004), Barcelona (2004–2009)
Segunda División (Spain): Leganés (1997–1998, loan)
Serie A (Italy): Inter Milan (2009–2011), Sampdoria (2015)
Russian Premier League: Anzhi Makhachkala (2011–2013)
Premier League (England): Chelsea (2013–2014), Everton (2014–2015)
Süper Lig (Türkiye): Antalyaspor (2015–2018), Konyaspor (2018)
Qatar Stars League (Qatar): Qatar SC (2018–2019)

One of Africa's greatest players, Samuel Eto'o became Mallorca's all-time leading scorer (seventy goals) in just five seasons, before joining Barcelona. There, he won seven trophies, including a sextuple. He also helped Inter Milan win six titles in two seasons, including a treble (2010). Eto'o earned 118 caps for Cameroon, playing in four World Cups and winning two African Cup of Nations (2000, 2002), finishing as top scorer twice (2006, 2008) for the latter tournament. He is Cameroon's all-time top scorer (fifty-six goals) as well as the highest-scoring African player in LaLiga history (162 goals).

Ada Hegerberg: Miss Champions

POSITION(S) Striker

TEAM(S) AND YEARS **Toppserien (Norway):** Kolbotn (2010–2011), Stabæk (2012–2013)
Frauen-Bundesliga (Germany): Turbine Potsdam (2013–2014)
Première Ligue (France): Lyon (2014–Present)

Ada Hegerberg's technical skills and innate goal instincts have made her one of the most recognizable names in soccer today. At age sixteen, she became the youngest female player to score a hat trick in Norway's top division. She joined Olympique Lyonnais in 2014, where she has helped the club win nineteen domestic titles and six Champions League trophies. Hegerberg has won one Ballon d'Or (2018) and finished as top scorer in the French top flight on three occasions. No female player has scored more than her sixty goals in Champions League action. Despite a five-year hiatus from Norway's national team, she has over ninety caps and fifty goals to her name.

Thierry Henry: King Henry

POSITION(S) Striker, Winger

TEAM(S) AND YEARS
Championnat de France Amateur: Monaco B (1994–1995)
Division 1 (France): Monaco (1994–1999)
Serie A (Italy): Juventus (1999)
Premier League (England): Arsenal (1999–2007; 2012, loan)
LaLiga (Spain): Barcelona (2007–2010)
Major League Soccer (US): New York Red Bulls (2010–2014)

Few players have played with the level of swagger that Thierry Henry projected. A winger-turned-striker, Henry had a signature move: to drift out wide before cutting in and beating goalkeepers to the far post. Henry won seven domestic titles with Arsenal, including completing a Premier League season undefeated, as well as two European Golden Shoes and the league's Golden Boot four times. He spent three seasons with Barcelona, where he won a sextuple. Henry earned 123 caps for France, scoring fifty-one goals and winning a World Cup (1998), a Euro (2000), and a Confederations Cup (2003). He is Arsenal's all-time leading goal scorer with 228 goals.

What's the Word?

European Golden Shoe

This award is given to the club player with the most goals scored during a European season.

Soccer's All-Time Super Scorers!

From thunderous headers to last-minute nail-biters, these legends have lit up the international stage with outstanding goals. Here's your ultimate scoreboard of the most prolific goal players—men and women who made the net ripple.

MEN'S SOCCER

These are the top five male players with the most goals in international matches. From Ronaldo's relentless drive to Messi's incredible mastery, these stars have made history with every strike.

- **CRISTIANO RONALDO:** 138 goals in 221 matches
- **LIONEL MESSI:** 112 goals in 193 matches
- **ALI DAEI:** 108 goals in 148 matches
- **SUNIL CHHETRI:** 94 goals in 151 matches
- **MOKHTAR DAHARI:** 89 goals in 142 matches

WOMEN'S SOCCER

These five women are the most prolific goal scorers in international soccer history. Whether it's Sinclair's unmatched consistency or Wambach's aerial dominance, these athletes have redefined excellence on the pitch.

- **CHRISTINE SINCLAIR:** 190 goals in 328 matches
- **ABBY WAMBACH:** 184 goals in 255 matches
- **MIA HAMM:** 158 goals in 276 matches
- **MAYSA JBARAH:** 137 goals in 133 matches
- **CARLI LLOYD:** 134 goals in 315 matches

Son Heung-min: Sensational

POSITION Winger, striker, Center-forward

TEAMS AND YEARS
Regionalliga Nord (Germany): Hamburger SV II (2009–2010)
Bundesliga (Germany): Hamburger SV (2010–2013), Bayer Leverkusen (2013–2015)
Premier League (England): Tottenham Hotspur (2015–2025)
MLS (US): Los Angeles FC (LAFC) (2025–Present)

Son Heung-min is making a strong case as one of the best Asian players of all time. During his time with Tottenham, he has helped the club win a UEFA Europa League title, while also claiming a Premier League Golden Boot. He is the highest-scoring Asian in Premier League history. Son has represented South Korea in three World Cups (2014, 2018, 2022), while leading them to a gold medal at the 2018 Asian Games and helping his nation finish as runners-up at the 2015 AFC Asian Cup. He has earned 133 caps and has scored fifty-one goals.

Zlatan Ibrahimović: The Lion

POSITION(S) Striker

TEAM(S) AND YEARS
Allsvenskan (Sweden): Malmö FF (1999–2001)
Eredivisie (Netherlands): Ajax (2001–2004)
Serie A (Italy): Juventus (2004–2006), Inter Milan (2006–2009), Milan (2009–2010, loan; 2011–2012, 2020–2023)
LaLiga (Spain): Barcelona (2009–2011)
Ligue 1 (France): Paris Saint-Germain (2012–2016)
Premier League (England): Manchester United (2016–2018)
Major League Soccer (US): Los Angeles Galaxy (2018–2019)

Zlatan Ibrahimović was never short of self-confidence and with good reason: Ibrahimović scored over 500 goals between 1999 and 2023 while winning thirty-two trophies from some of the most prestigious places, including the Spanish, Italian, English, French, and Dutch leagues. He represented Sweden at two World Cups and four Euros. In all, Ibrahimović earned 122 caps and scored sixty-two goals, more than any other Swede. He is one of the greatest players not to win the Champions League.

Harry Kane: The Hurricane

POSITION(S) Striker

TEAM(S) AND YEARS **Premier League (England):** Tottenham Hotspur (2009–2023), Norwich City (2012–2013, loan)
League One (England): Leyton Orient (2011, loan)
EFL Championship (England): Millwall (2012, loan), Leicester City (2013, loan)
Bundesliga (Germany): Bayern Munich (2023–Present)

Despite not being as athletic as some of his contemporaries, Harry Kane has such composure during the final third of a game that he became one of the highest-scoring strikers in recent years. He is Tottenham Hotspur's all-time top scorer (280 goals) and a three-time Premier League Golden Boot winner. He joined Bayern Munich in 2023 and won the European Golden Shoe in his first season there before winning the first club trophy of his career the following year. He is also England's all-time leading scorer with seventy-one goals in 105 appearances and has played in two World Cups and three Euros. He won Golden Boot honors at the 2018 World Cup and 2020 Euro.

Sam Kerr: Thunder from Down Under

POSITION(S) Striker

TEAM(S) AND YEARS **W-League (Australia):** Perth Glory (2008–2011, 2014–2019), Sydney FC (2012–2014)
National Women's Soccer League (US): Western New York Flash (2013–2014), Sky Blue (2015–2017), Chicago Red Stars (2018–2019)
Women's Super League (England): Chelsea (2020–Present)

Sam Kerr's ability to score goals and work well with her teammates near the goal has made her one of the best strikers in recent years. With fourteen club trophies throughout her career, Kerr has finished as her league's top scorer on seven occasions and is the only female soccer player to have done so in three different leagues. Australia's captain and all-time leading female goal scorer, Kerr has won the AFC Women's Asian Cup (2010) and played in four World Cups.

Robert Lewandowski: Lewangoalski

POSITION(S) Striker

TEAM(S) AND YEARS **IV liga (Poland):** Delta Warsaw (2005)
III liga (Poland): Legia Warsaw II (2005–2006)
Klasa A (Poland): Znicz II Pruszków (2006)
II liga (Poland): Znicz Pruszków (2006–2008)
Ekstraklasa (Poland): Lech Poznań (2008–2010)
Bundesliga (Germany): Borussia Dortmund (2010–2014), Bayern Munich (2014–2022)
LaLiga (Spain): Barcelona (2022–Present)

Robert Lewandowski's longevity at the top of the game is a credit to his work ethic and self-discipline. Lewandowski became a superstar during his time in the Bundesliga with Borussia Dortmund and Bayern Munich. In twelve seasons, he won twenty-three trophies, including a sextuple with Munich in 2020. A two-time European Golden Shoe winner, he was also the top scorer in the Bundesliga on seven occasions. Lewandowski has played in two World Cups and three Euros. He is Poland's all-time leading goal scorer with eighty-five goals in 158 appearances, and over 700 goals scored throughout his career.

Kylian Mbappé: Lightning and Thunder

POSITION(S) Winger, Striker

TEAM(S) AND YEARS **Championnat de France Amateur:** Monaco II (2015–2016)
Ligue 1 (France): Monaco (2015–2018),
Paris Saint-Germain (2017–2018, loan; 2018–2024)
LaLiga (Spain): Real Madrid (2024–Present)

Quick as lightning and devastating as thunder, Kylian Mbappé could retire tomorrow and still have accomplished more than most players! At twenty-six years old, he has already won twenty trophies, including a World Cup. Mbappé spent seven seasons with Paris Saint-Germain, winning everything at the domestic level while becoming the club's all-time leading scorer (256 goals).

Mbappé has already earned ninety caps and scored fifty goals for France. In 2018, he earned Best Young Player honors as France claimed its second World Cup. During the 2022 World Cup, Mbappé scored eight goals—including a hat trick in the final—leading France to a second-place finish and claiming Golden Boot and Silver Ball honors.

Lionel Messi: The Atomic Flea

POSITION(S) Winger, Center forward, Attacking midfielder

TEAM(S) AND YEARS **Tercera División (Spain):** Barcelona C (2003–2004)
Segunda División B (Spain): Barcelona B (2004–2005)
LaLiga (Spain): Barcelona (2004–2021)
Ligue 1 (France): Paris Saint-Germain (2021–2023)
Major League Soccer (US): Inter Miami (2023–Present)

Slight in stature but larger than life on the field, Lionel Messi is nicknamed the "Atomic Flea" due to his diminutive size and extraordinary skills. A complete forward who excels at dribbling, scoring, and passing, he is Barcelona's greatest player. He holds club records for most goals (672), assists (305), appearances (778), and trophies (35). Messi was pivotal in Barcelona's sextuple (2009) and treble (2014–2015). He was the top scorer of the Champions League six times and the top scorer of LaLiga a record eight times.

Messi is Argentina's all-time leader in goals (112), assists (58), and appearances (191). He has played in five World Cups, winning the 2022 Cup, while earning Golden Ball honors twice (2014, 2022). Messi has also won the Copa América twice (2021, 2023), was named the tournament's Golden Ball recipient twice (2015, 2021), and finished as top scorer once (2021).

The Stats Behind the Legend

- **Most team trophies (45)**
- **Most European Golden Shoes (6)**
- **Most goals scored in a calendar year (91 goals, 2012)**
- **Most goals (474) and assists (106) in LaLiga action**
- **Most goals (26) in *El Clásico* matches**

FOOTBALL UNITES the World
FIFA
10

Alex Morgan: Baby Horse

POSITION(S) Center forward, Striker

TEAM(S) AND YEARS **Women's Premier Soccer League (US):** West Coast (2008–2009), California Storm (2010)
USL W-League (US): Pali Blues (2010), Seattle Sounders Women (2012)
Women's Professional Soccer (US): Western New York Flash (2011)
National Women's Soccer League (US): Portland Thorns (2013–2015), Orlando Pride (2016, 2017–2020, 2021), San Diego Wave (2022–2024)
Division 1 Féminine (France): Lyon (2017)
FA WSL (England): Tottenham Hotspur (2020)

Alex Morgan was so fast when she joined pro soccer at twenty-two that her teammates nicknamed her "Baby Horse." She quickly became one of America's greatest players. Morgan won seven club trophies, including the Champions League, but she's best known for her success with the US national team. She earned 224 caps and scored 124 goals. She also won two World Cups (2015, 2019), an Olympic gold medal (2012), and three Concacaf Women's Championships (2014, 2018, 2022).

Birgit Prinz: Difference Maker

POSITION(S) Striker

TEAM(S) AND YEARS **Frauen- Bundesliga (Germany):** FSV Frankfurt (1993–1998), 1. FFC Frankfurt (1998–2002, 2003–2011)
Women's United Soccer Association (US): Carolina Courage (2002–2003)

When Birgit Prinz scored the game-winning goal seconds before full time in her debut with Germany's senior team at just sixteen years old, it became evident she was poised for greatness. Nearly undefendable in her prime, Prinz won three consecutive FIFA World Player of the Year awards (2003–2005), as well as nineteen domestic titles and three Champions Leagues at club level. She represented Germany at five World Cups, winning back-to-back trophies in the 2003 and 2007 tournaments. She took home Golden Ball and Golden Boot honors in 2003 and Silver Ball honors in 2007. Prinz also helped Germany win five consecutive Euros (1995, 1997, 2001, 2005, 2009). She is Germany's all-time leader in goals (128) and appearances (214).

Christian Pulisic: Captain America

POSITION(S) Winger, Attacking midfielder

TEAM(S) AND YEARS **Bundesliga (Germany):** Borussia Dortmund (2016–2019, 2019, loan)
Premier League (England): Chelsea (2019–2023)
Serie A (Italy): Milan (2023–Present)

A constant scoring threat whether playing as a winger or playmaker for club or country, Christian Pulisic is already one of the best Americans to play the game. Pulisic made his professional debut at seventeen years old and became the first American to play in and win a Champions League final at twenty-two years old with Chelsea. Notably, he has won at least one trophy for all three clubs he has played for. Pulisic has earned over seventy caps for the US and scored more than thirty goals, helping the US win three Concacaf Nations League trophies.

Wayne Rooney: The English Bulldog

POSITION(S) Striker, Center forward, Attacking midfielder

TEAM(S) AND YEARS **Premier League (England):** Everton (2002–2004, 2017–2018), Manchester United (2004–2017)
Major League Soccer (US): D.C. United (2018–2019)
English Football League Championship (England): Derby County (2020–2021)

Known for his stunning goals and relentless work rate, Wayne Rooney burst onto the scene at sixteen years old before establishing himself as one of the best strikers in the Premier League. Rooney won sixteen trophies in twelve seasons at Manchester United, netting 253 goals to become the club's all-time leading scorer. Rooney was also a prominent player for England, making 120 appearances and scoring fifty-three goals, while playing in three World Cups and three Euros.

Cristiano Ronaldo: Mr. Champions

POSITION(S) Winger, Striker

TEAM(S) AND YEARS
Segunda Divisão B (Portugal): Sporting CP B (2002–2003)
Primeira Liga (Portugal): Sporting CP (2002–2003)
Premier League (England): Manchester United (2003–2009, 2021–2022)
LaLiga (Spain): Real Madrid (2009–2018)
Serie A (Italy): Juventus (2018–2021)
Saudi Pro League: Al-Nassr (2023–Present)

Perhaps no other player has shone as brightly under the Champions League lights as Cristiano Ronaldo. A winger-turned-striker, Ronaldo boasts the records, trophy case, athleticism, and longevity to rival any other athlete in the history of sports. A legend at both Manchester United and Real Madrid, Ronaldo has won thirty-one trophies at club level, including five Champions League trophies. Notably, no one has scored more goals (141), provided more assists (forty-four), or played more matches (187) in Champions League action than Ronaldo. He has finished as the top scorer of the Champions League seven times, while also winning four European Golden Shoes.

He is the only player to finish as top scorer in the Premier League, LaLiga, and Serie A. Ronaldo is a stalwart with Portugal, whom he has represented since 2003, and he played a pivotal role as his nation won its first international trophy during Euro 2016. He also led Portugal to win two UEFA Nations League titles (2019, 2025). He has scored more goals (138) and earned more caps (221) in international soccer than any other male player. Ronaldo is Portugal's greatest player.

QUICK KICKS

Ronaldo is the only player in history to have scored in five World Cups (2006, 2010, 2014, 2018, 2022).

7
RESPECT
7

Mohamed Salah: The Pharaoh of Anfield

POSITION(S) Winger, Center forward

TEAM(S) AND YEARS **Egyptian Premier League:** Al-Mokawloon (2010–2012),
Swiss Super League: Basel (2012–2014)
Premier League (England): Chelsea (2014–2016), Liverpool (2017–Present)
Serie A (Italy): Fiorentina (2015, loan), Roma (2015–2016, loan; 2016–2017)

Mohamed Salah joined Liverpool in 2017 and has scored nearly 250 goals, helping the club win nine trophies, including a Champions League. He's won the Premier League Golden Boot, a joint-record four times. For Egypt, he's earned one hundred caps, scored sixty goals, and played in one World Cup. Salah led Egypt to two African Cup of Nations finals and, as of 2025, is the Premier League's highest-scoring foreign player.

Alexis Sánchez: The Wonder Boy

POSITION(S) Winger, Center forward

TEAM(S) AND YEARS **Primera División:** Cobreloa (2005–2006), Colo-Colo (2006–2007, loan)
Serie A (Italy): Udinese (2006–2011, 2024–2025), Inter Milan (2019–2020, loan; 2020–2022, 2023–2024)
Primera División (Argentina): River Plate (2007–2008)
LaLiga (Spain): Barcelona (2011–2014), Sevilla (2025–Present)
Premier League (England): Arsenal (2014–2018), Manchester United (2018–2020)
Ligue 1 (France): Marseille (2022–2023)

Alexis Sánchez made his pro debut at fifteen and has played for nine clubs, winning sixteen trophies. He was key to Chile's golden generation and his country's first international title, scoring the winning penalty in the 2015 Copa América final. He helped Chile defend the title again in 2016, earning the Golden Ball. Sánchez is Chile's all-time leader in goals (fifty-one) and appearances (168), making him one of the country's greatest soccer stars.

Andriy Shevchenko: The Eastern Wind

POSITION(S) Striker

TEAM(S) AND YEARS **First League (Ukraine):** Dynamo-2 Kyiv (1993–1996)
Premier League (Ukraine): Dynamo Kyiv (1993–1999, 2009–2012)
Serie A (Italy): Milan (1999–2006, 2008–2009, loan)
Premier League (England): Chelsea (2006–2009)

Andriy Shevchenko was a fast and physical striker who became a superstar at Milan, where he won five trophies, including the Champions League. He also won a Ballon d'Or (2004) and finished as Serie A's top scorer twice. Shevchenko made 111 appearances for Ukraine, captaining the side in the 2006 World Cup, leading his nation to the quarterfinals in their first appearance at the tournament. He is Ukraine's all-time leading goal scorer with forty-eight goals. Shevchenko is Ukraine's greatest player.

Christine Sinclair: Record-Setter

POSITION(S) Striker

TEAM(S) AND YEARS **Women's Premier Soccer League (US):** Vancouver Angels (2000)
USL W-League (US): Vancouver Breakers (2001–2002), Vancouver Whitecaps (2006–2008)
Women's Professional Soccer (US): Gold Pride (2009–2010), Western New York Flash (2011)
National Women's Soccer League (US): Portland Thorns (2013–2024)

When Christine Sinclair debuted with Canada's senior team at age sixteen, few could have predicted the heights she would reach. In addition to her eleven trophies at club level, Sinclair led Canada to win the 2010 Concacaf Women's Championship, an Olympic gold medal (2021), and two bronze medals (2012, 2016). She also helped Canada reach the semifinals of the 2003 World Cup, the nation's best finish at the tournament. Sinclair's 190 goals for Canada make her the highest scorer in international women's soccer, while her 331 appearances make her the most-capped Canadian female player. She is one of two female players to score at five World Cups.

Luis Suárez: The Gunslinger

POSITION(S) Striker, Winger

TEAM(S) AND YEARS **Primera División:** Nacional (2005–2006, 2022–2023)
Eredivisie (Netherlands): Groningen (2006–2007), Ajax (2007–2011)
Premier League (England): Liverpool (2011–2014)
LaLiga (Spain): Barcelona (2014–2020), Atlético Madrid (2020–2022)
Campeonato Brasileiro Série A: Grêmio (2023–2024)
Major League Soccer (US): Inter Miami (2024–Present)

Luis Suárez is one of the best forwards in the modern era. Suárez has been the top scorer in the Eredivisie, the Premier League, and LaLiga, while winning twenty-four trophies. While with Barcelona, he won thirteen trophies, including a treble. Suárez has earned 143 caps for Uruguay. In 2011, he made six goal contributions to help Uruguay win Copa América, while winning Most Valuable Player honors. He is Uruguay's all-time leading goal scorer with sixty-nine goals. Notably, Suárez twice outscored both Lionel Messi and Cristiano Ronaldo to claim two European Golden Shoes.

Francesco Totti: The Eighth King of Rome

POSITION(S) Center forward, Striker, Attacking midfielder

TEAM(S) AND YEARS **Serie A (Italy):** Roma (1993–2017)

Francesco Totti spent his entire twenty-five-year career playing for Roma. He won five trophies—including Roma's first Serie A title in nineteen years—along with a European Golden Shoe and Serie A top scorer honors. He was named to Italy's 2006 World Cup squad despite being inactive for three months prior due to injuries. Totti went on to play every match and provide five goal contributions as Italy secured its fourth World Cup. In all, he made fifty-eight appearances for Italy and retired from Roma as the player with the most club goals (307) and appearances (786). For all the kings and emperors in Rome's history, none was as beloved as Totti.

Marta Vieira da Silva: A Rainha

POSITION(S) Center forward, Striker

TEAM(S) AND YEARS **Campeonato Brasileiro de Futebol Feminino (Brazil):** Vasco da Gama (2000–2002)
Campeonato Mineiro Feminino (Brazil): Santa Cruz (2002–2004)
Damallsvenskan (Sweden): Umeå IK (2004–2008), Tyresö (2012–2014), Rosengård (2014–2017)
Women's Professional Soccer (US): Los Angeles Sol (2009), San Francisco Gold Pride (2010), Western New York Flash (2011)
Copa do Brasil de Futebol Feminino: Santos (2009–2010, loan; 2011)
National Women's Soccer League (US): Orlando Pride (2017–Present)

When it comes to Brazilian women's soccer, Marta Vieira da Silva stands out as one of the greatest. Whether she's scoring or setting up goals, her talent on the field is undeniable. She's known as *A Rainha*, which means "The Queen"—a name she's definitely earned through years of incredible play.

Marta has played in Europe, North America, and South America at club level, winning fifteen trophies and finishing as her league's top scorer on six occasions. She has won six Best FIFA Women's World Player of the Year awards (2006, 2007, 2008, 2009, 2010, 2018)—four more than the next closest player. She is also Brazil's all-time leading scorer, with more than 120 goals in over 180 international appearances. During her time with the national team, she led Brazil to four Copa América Femenina titles and played in a World Cup final (2007) and three Olympics finals (2004, 2008, 2024). Marta won the Golden Ball and Golden Boot at the 2007 World Cup. She was the first player of any gender to score at five World Cups (2003, 2007, 2011, 2015, 2019). She retired from international duty in 2024.

Women on the Field

- The first FIFA Women's World Cup started sixty-one years after the men's. It was held in 1991 in China.
- Marta Vieira da Silva is the all-time World Cup top scorer, with seventeen goals.
- Formiga, the Brazilian midfielder, is the only woman player to have played in seven World Cups and seven Olympics.

Abby Wambach: Air Wambach

POSITION(S) Striker

TEAM(S) AND YEARS **Women's United Soccer Association (US):** Washington Freedom (2002–2003)
Women's Premier Soccer League (US): Ajax America Women (2005)
Women's Professional Soccer (US): Washington Freedom (2009–2010), Boca Raton MagicJack (2011)
National Women's Soccer League (US): Western New York Flash (2013–2014)

No striker has been more dominant in the air for the United States than Abby Wambach. Standing at 5'11", Wambach was renowned for winning aerial duels and getting her head on the end of crosses. Wambach represented the US at four World Cups, helping the Americans win the 2015 tournament, finish as runners-up in 2011, and finish third twice (2003, 2007). She earned a Silver Ball and Bronze Boot honors during the 2011 tournament. Wambach also helped the US win gold at the 2004 and 2012 Olympics. She was named the 2012 FIFA Women's Player of the Year, becoming the first American in a decade to win the award. Wambach earned 255 caps for the US and scored 184 goals. She is the all-time leading goal scorer for the US women's national team.

Mini Quiz: Goal Superstars

Let's see how much you know about forwards!

1. What is the main job of a center forward?

- **A.** To score goals and lead attacks
- **B.** To stop goals
- **C.** To kick the ball

2. Who is the all-time top scorer in men's international soccer?

- **A.** Cristiano Ronaldo
- **B.** Lionel Messi
- **C.** Erling Haaland

3. Who holds the most World Cup titles?

- **A.** Cristiano Ronaldo
- **B.** Lionel Messi
- **C.** Neymar da Silva Santos Jr.

Answer Key: A., A., B.

Chapter 6

More Global Legends

As we know by now, soccer is popular all over the world. With so many players over the years, it's impossible to know all of them. Since the sport is so popular worldwide, there are players whom you may not have heard of who are legends in other parts of the world, including Asia, Africa, Central America, and the Middle East. I've compiled a list of some of these amazing legends, each of whom brought their own unique style to the game. Some of them may come from small countries, but the impact of their legacy is as big as it gets.

QUICK KICKS

There is evidence to show that women were playing soccer in ancient China, as far back as 22 BCE. This means that women have been on the field for thousands of years!

From inspiring goal scorers to midfield geniuses, these players have inspired millions and shaped the identity of soccer in their regions. Whether you're a casual fan or a soccer super-fan, get ready to discover greatness across continents. Let's see how many of these legends you know!

Nadine Angerer of Germany tries to stop a goal at the 2015 FIFA Women's World Cup.

Ali Daei: Mr. Goal

POSITION(S) Striker

TEAM(S) AND YEARS **Tehran League (Iran):** Bank Tejarat (1990–1994)
Azadegan League (Iran): Persepolis (1994–1996)
Qatar Stars League (Qatar): Al Sadd (1996–1997)
Bundesliga (Germany): Arminia Bielefeld (1997–1998), Bayern Munich (1998–1999), Hertha BSC (1999–2002)
UAE Pro League (United Arab Emirates): Al Shabab (2002–2003)
Iran Pro League (Iran): Persepolis (2003–2004), Saba Battery (2004–2006), Saipa (2006–2007)

A forward who made use of his 6'4" frame to score from headers, Ali Daei was a pioneer of Middle Eastern soccer. He won six club trophies during his career, including a domestic double with Bayern Munich. With 108 goals in 148 appearances, Daei is Iran's all-time record scorer and played in three World Cups. Until Cristiano Ronaldo broke his record in 2021, no male player had scored more goals at the international level than Ali Daei.

What's the Word?

Panenka

Panenka is a type of penalty kick in which the player gently lobs the ball, so it lands in the center of the goal rather than kicking it to the right or left. It is named after Antonín Panenka, a Czech player who popularized the technique.

Nadine Angerer: The Pillar

POSITION(S) Goalkeeper

TEAM(S) AND YEARS **Frauen-Bundesliga (Germany):** 1. FC Nürnberg (1995–1996), FC Wacker München (1996–1999), FC Bayern Munich (1999–2001), 1. FFC Turbine Potsdam (2001–2007), 1. FFC Frankfurt (2009–2013)
Damallsvenskan (Sweden): Djurgårdens IF (2008)
A-League Women (Australia): Brisbane Roar (2013–2014)
National Women's Soccer League (US): Portland Thorns FC (2014–2015)

Nadine Angerer's twenty-five-year career included winning two World Cups (2003, 2007) and five Women's Euro titles with Germany. Angerer also won seven trophies at the club level, but it's her time with the German women's national team that she is most remembered for. In addition to being named Best Goalkeeper at the 2007 World Cup, she won the 2013 FIFA Women's World Player of the Year award, becoming the first and only goalkeeper to earn this honor.

QUICK KICKS

During the 2007 Women's World Cup, Nadine Angerer played 540 minutes without conceding a goal, a World Cup record she shares with Hope Solo.

Jorge González: El Mágico

POSITION(S) Center forward, Attacking midfielder

TEAM(S) AND YEARS **Primera División de Fútbol (El Salvador):** ANTEL (1975–1976), Independiente Nacional (1976–1977), FAS (1977–1982, 1991–1999)
LaLiga (Spain): Cádiz (1982–1984, 1986–1991), Valladolid (1985)

Jorge González, better known as *El Mágico* (The Magic One) because of his magical dribbles, is widely regarded as El Salvador's greatest player. During his time at FAS, he helped the club win six titles, including a Champions Cup. González's performances at the 1982 World Cup caught the eye of European teams, and he signed with Cádiz that year. He spent seven seasons with Cádiz, becoming one of their most legendary players. González scored twenty-one goals in sixty-two appearances for El Salvador.

Team Swap!

When Players Change National Teams

A long time ago, soccer players could play for more than one country if they wanted. But in 2004, FIFA made a new rule: if a player played for one country as a kid, they could switch to a different country when they got older—but only once, and only if they asked before turning twenty-one.

Today, the rule says that players under twenty-one who have two nationalities can change which country they play for if they've played fewer than three games for their first country, or if they haven't played for that country in three years. But they can't switch if they've already played in a big international tournament for their first country.

Why did FIFA make this change? Well, they did this to keep things fair. Before this rule, teams would recruit players that had no connection to them, just to build stronger teams. This new rule gives players a chance to pick which country they would like to represent. This is especially helpful for players who have two nationalities or who moved to a new country and gives them a chance to pick the team they feel more connected to.

Hidetoshi Nakata: The Sparkplug

POSITION(S) Attacking midfielder, Central midfielder

TEAM(S) AND YEARS **J1 League (Japan):** Bellmare Hiratsuka (1995–1998)
Serie A (Italy): Perugia (1998–2000), Roma (2000–2001), Parma (2001–2004), Bologna (2004, loan), Fiorentina (2004–2006)
Premier League (England): Bolton Wanderers (2005–2006, loan)

With his endless stamina and hard work ethic, Hidetoshi Nakata was able to liven things up for every team he played for. The biggest Asian player at the turn of the century, Nakata played in every one of Japan's matches in its first three World Cups. He spent a bulk of his career in Serie A and was a member of the historic Roma side that won the league in 2001.

QUICK KICKS

After Hidetoshi Nakata retired from soccer, he modeled for big fashion brands like Calvin Klein.

Perpetua Nkwocha: The Green Eagle

POSITION(S) Attacking midfielder, Center forward

TEAM(S) AND YEARS **Damallsvenskan (Sweden):** Sunnanå SK (2007–2014)

Perpetua Nkwocha could be considered the greatest female African player of all time. On her best day, Nkwocha was impossible to stop. She scored eighty goals in ninety-nine appearances for Nigeria, helping the side win five Women's African Cup of Nations titles (2002, 2004, 2006, 2010, 2014) while finishing as top scorer on three consecutive occasions (2002, 2004, 2006). In 2004, she scored four goals in the final of the tournament, also earning Golden Ball honors.

Gheorghe Hagi: The Maradona of the Carpathians

POSITION(S) Attacking midfielder

TEAM(S) AND YEARS **Divizia A (Romania):** Constanța (1982–1983), Sportul Studențesc (1983–1987), Steaua București (1987–1990)
LaLiga (Spain): Real Madrid (1990–1992), Barcelona (1994–1996)
Serie A (Italy): Brescia (1992–1994)
1.Lig (Türkiye): Galatasaray (1996–2001)

A crafty playmaker with an eye for the goal, Gheorghe Hagi was known as the "Maradona of the Carpathians." Hagi played for some of the biggest clubs in Europe, winning eighteen trophies during a storied career. He also made 124 appearances for Romania, scoring thirty-five goals. He played in three World Cups and three Euros. Notably, during the 1994 World Cup, Hagi scored five goals, helping Romania reach the quarterfinals.

Mini Quiz: Global Greats

Can you guess which player holds what achievements? Let's find out!

1. Who held the record for the most international goals scored by a male player until Cristiano Ronaldo broke it in 2021?

   A. Pelé
   B. Lionel Messi
   C. Ali Daei

2. What unique achievement does Nadine Angerer hold as a goalkeeper?

   A. She invented the Panenka penalty kick
   B. She won the FIFA Women's World Player of the Year award
   C. She played in five World Cups

3. How many Women's African Cup of Nations titles did Perpetua Nkwocha win with Nigeria?

   A. Two
   B. Four
   C. Five

Answer Key: C., B., C.

ETIHAD
AIRWAYS
40

Chapter 7

Rising Stars
The Future of Soccer

Just as soccer tactics evolve, the faces of soccer change. From Pelé to Cruyff, from Maradona to Zidane, and from Ronaldinho to Messi, the torch is constantly being passed from one generation to the next. Far away from the brightness of stadium lights, new stars are beginning to rise each day while others fade. Even as we speak, there's probably a kid somewhere out there who will be scoring the game-winning goal in a World Cup one day. Here are some of the rising stars in soccer who are beginning to write their own story.

QUICK KICKS

The youngest player to win the Golden Ball at a World Cup is Ronaldo Nazário de Lima, who won the award in 1998, when he was just 21.

Erling Haaland of Manchester City in action during the Premier League match between Manchester City FC and Ipswich Town FC.

Jude Bellingham: Jude Ballon d'Or

POSITION(S) Central midfielder

TEAM(S) AND YEARS **EFL Championship (England):** Birmingham City (2019–2020)
Bundesliga (Germany): Borussia Dortmund (2020–2023)
LaLiga (Spain): Real Madrid (2023–Present)

Sometimes it's hard to believe that Jude Bellingham is only twenty-one years old. In just six seasons, he has already made a case for being among the greatest midfielders of his generation. During his first season with Real Madrid, Bellingham won five trophies, including the Champions League. A versatile midfielder, he is nearing fifty caps for England and has already played in a Euro final. Fans who believe he is destined to win great things have nicknamed him "Jude Ballon d'Or."

Erling Haaland: The Terminator

POSITION(S) Striker

TEAM(S) AND YEARS **3. divisjon (Norway):** Bryne 2 (2015–2016), Molde 2 (2017)
1. divisjon (Norway): Bryne (2016)
Eliteserien (Norway): Molde (2017–2019)
Austrian Bundesliga: Red Bull Salzburg (2019–2020)
Bundesliga (Germany): Borussia Dortmund (2020–2022)
Premier League (England): Manchester City (2022–Present)

At just twenty-five years old, Erling Haaland has already won nine trophies, including a sextuple with Manchester City. Individually, he has won a European Golden Shoe and two Premier League Golden Boots. A natural goal-scoring machine, Haaland holds the record for most goals in a single Premier League season (thirty-six). He has scored over fifty-one goals in forty-six appearances for Norway. He's been given multiple nicknames to reflect his speed and power including: "The Terminator," "The Striking King," and "Daemon."

Trinity Rodman: Triple Espresso

POSITION(S) Winger

TEAM(S) AND YEARS **National Women's Soccer League (US):** Washington Spirit (2021–Present)

In 2021, at eighteen years old, Trinity Rodman became the youngest player to be selected in the National Women's Soccer League draft when she was chosen by the Washington Spirit, with whom she has won two domestic trophies. Rodman has earned almost fifty caps with the United States. She has won an Olympic gold medal (2024) and the Concacaf W Gold Cup (2024) while also playing in one World Cup. Her nickname is one she shares with fellow soccer stars: Sophia Smith and Mallory Swanson—showcasing the trio's attacking power.

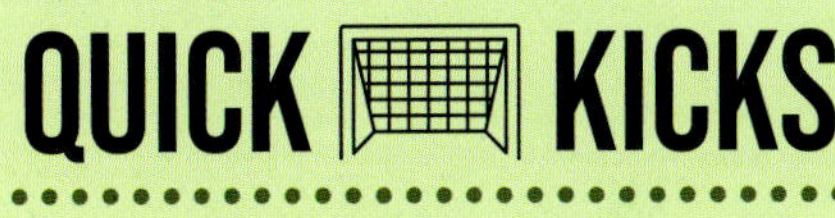

Trinity Rodman is the daughter of former basketball player Dennis Rodman.

Lamine Yamal: Ryan

POSITION(S) Winger

TEAM(S) AND YEARS **Primera Federación (Spain):** Barcelona B (2023)
LaLiga (Spain): Barcelona (2023–Present)

Lamine Yamal's rise to fame has been so quick that it's hard to keep up. Since making his professional debut at fifteen years old in 2023, he has become an undisputed starter for Barcelona, helping the club win four trophies. Since his breakout performance at Euro 2024, where he scored one goal and provided four assists to help Spain win the tournament, he has cemented his place as a starter for his country. Yamal was seventeen years old when he won the Euro 2024, making him the youngest male player to win an international trophy with his national team. His nickname "Ryan" reflects his humor and humility—when fans didn't recognize him, he jokingly gave a fake name. It's since become a playful nickname among his fans.

Barbra Banda: Bex

POSITION(S) Striker

TEAM(S) AND YEARS **Lusaka League (Zambia):** Green Buffaloes (2016–2018)
Liga F (Spain): Logroño (2018–2020)
Chinese Women's Super League: Shanghai Shengli (2020–2023)
National Women's Soccer League (US): Orlando Pride (2024–Present)

Fast, strong, and intelligent, Barbra Banda is a handful for defenders and goalkeepers alike. A proven goal scorer, Banda scored eighteen goals in thirteen matches to win the Chinese Women's Super League Golden Boot. She joined Orlando Pride in 2024, leading the club to a domestic double. At twenty-five years old, she has already earned sixty-three caps for Zambia, scoring fifty-seven goals and playing in one World Cup. She is the top scorer in Africa's Olympic women's soccer, and she became the first player—male or female—to score back-to-back hat tricks in Olympic soccer history in the Tokyo 2020 Olympics.

QUICK KICKS

Before becoming the soccer legend that she is today, Banda was a professional boxer in Zambia.

Mini Quiz: Future Stars

Let's test your knowledge on these rising soccer stars!

1. Which player shares a nickname with two other players?

A. Trinity Rodman
B. Erling Haaland
C. Barbra Banda

2. Who was the youngest male player to win an international trophy with his national team?

A. Pelé
B. Lamine Yamal
C. Gheorghe Hagi

3. Who won five trophies in his first season playing for Real Madrid?

A. Jude Bellingham
B. Fabio Cannavaro
C. Keylor Navas

Answer Key: A., B., A.

L.F.C.
Standard Chartered
11

Chapter 8

Soccer Legacies Beyond the Field

Athletes have always been viewed as role models for the youth, and soccer players are no exception. However, while some soccer players serve as role models because of their discipline and dedication to the sport, others are role models for reasons that extend beyond the field.

The players in this section have taken it upon themselves to fight for causes they believe in, using their platform to serve a greater purpose. While the causes differ, you will notice a familiar pattern: Every player in this section tried, or is trying, to make the world a better place. However, these are not the only players that have made an impact outside of the field; this is a starting list of outstanding players making a difference in the world.

While soccer players are trying to make the world a better place, FIFA is also making progress in making the game fair and fun for everyone. They've made some good changes to help people feel included, but there's still more to do to make sure everyone gets treated equally on and off the field.

Mohamed Salah of Liverpool celebrates scoring a goal during the 2024 Premier League match between Southampton FC and Liverpool FC.

Stanley Matthews's Anti-Apartheid Efforts

In 1975, almost a decade after retiring, Stanley Matthews went to Soweto, South Africa, to establish a youth soccer team made up of all-Black players called Stan's Men during the middle of apartheid. Apartheid was a system used in South Africa where laws separated people based on their race. Black South Africans were not allowed to live, go to school, or even play sports in the same places as white South Africans.

Matthews had seen the potential of the young Black players and believed they deserved the same opportunities as anyone else. At one point, his players expressed their desire to go to Brazil, which they viewed as the soccer capital of the world. Through his connections, Matthews secured sponsors who covered not only a trip to Brazil, but also uniforms for the players. During the trip, the players met legends Pelé and Zico, ensuring it was a journey they would never forget. Matthews's efforts during the height of apartheid left a lasting mark on his players, with many of them going on to establish their own academies.

Pelé: Champion and Global Ambassador

In addition to all of his accomplishments on the field, Pelé was notorious for embodying the spirit of unity that comes with soccer. After he retired from the sport in 1977, Pelé focused on promoting the sport's values and advocating for causes such as world peace and international children's rights. Pelé served as an ambassador for international sports organizations such as FIFA and the International Olympic Committee and nongovernmental organizations such as the United Nations Children's Emergency Fund. In 2018, he founded the Pelé Foundation, which aims to help in the global fight for education and fights against poverty and hunger.

QUICK KICKS

In 1999, Pelé was named Athlete of the Century by the International Olympic Committee. Although he never participated in any Olympic Games, given his contributions to the sport on and off the field, the committee believed he embodied the Olympic values needed to win.

Rashford's Efforts Against Child Hunger

Marcus Rashford, an English forward who has played for Manchester United and the England national team, grew up in a single-parent household, with his mother having to work multiple jobs. After becoming a professional player, Rashford began working with different nonprofits to raise awareness about child hunger. On June 15, 2020, he wrote an open letter to the United Kingdom government, asking it to help end child poverty. A day later, the government announced that it would extend free school meals into summer vacation. Boris Johnson, prime minister at the time, credited Rashford for his contributions to raising awareness around the topic.

Kicking Goals and Becoming President

George Weah, a center forward from Liberia, is the only African player to ever win the Ballon d'Or. After retiring from the game, he went on to become the president of his country.

Following his retirement in 2002, Weah became involved in politics. He founded the Congress for Democratic Change political party in 2005 and ran for president that year but was unsuccessful. In 2014, he was elected to Liberia's senate, representing Montserrado County. Three years later, Weah ran for president, winning over 60 percent of the votes and becoming the first former professional soccer player to become president of a nation.

Although many people were excited when George Weah became president, his time in office later faced criticism about how things were run, and he didn't win re-election. Still, his journey from soccer star to president was a big and historic achievement that inspired people around the world.

Rapinoe's Fight for Equality

Megan Rapinoe will be remembered as much for her quality on the pitch as for her activism off it. Few players used their platform to speak about social justice issues to the degree Rapinoe did. Throughout her career, she drew attention to systemic racism and advocated for gender and pay equity, LGBTQ+ rights, and voter rights. Rapinoe was pivotal in creating a historic, first-of-its-kind collective bargaining agreement between the US Soccer Federation and the US Women's National Team Players Association that ensured, among other things, equal pay for its players. In 2022, the United States government recognized Rapinoe's advocacy efforts when she was awarded the Presidential Medal of Freedom.

Goals Outside the Net

From soccer players to global icons, these are some additional global players that have made an impact outside of the field, making history in incredible ways.

- **Estefanía Banini**, a talented midfielder from Argentina is often called the "Female Messi" because of her amazing footwork. In 2019, she was removed from Argentina's women's national team after speaking out about unfair treatment, but her return in 2022 marked a big step forward for women's soccer in Argentina.
- **Franz Beckenbauer**, a German defender, was famous for his leadership. He later became a successful coach, even managing his old team, Bayern Munich.
- **Mohamed Salah** is an Egyptian soccer superstar and a real-life hero in his hometown, where he built schools and a hospital. Proud of his Muslim faith, he often prays after scoring, and his popularity has helped inspire kindness and acceptance of Muslims in Liverpool. He's so loved that fans even sing songs about him!
- **Asisat Oshoala** is a Nigerian soccer star and five-time African Women Footballer of the Year. She started the Asisat Oshoala Foundation to help girls in Nigeria play soccer and go to school.
- **Marta Vieira da Silva**, a soccer star from Brazil, is often called one of the best female players ever. In 2018, she became a UN Women Goodwill Ambassador, using her voice to support girls and show they can be strong, skilled, and awesome in sports.

Breaking Barriers

With soccer's global popularity, you might think there isn't much it can do but continue to grow. But, as in any other sport, with growth comes growing pains, of which soccer has had its fair share. While the sport has overcome some of its issues, there are different growing pains that it must still address. As you learn about them in this section, consider how you can do your part.

The Rise of Women's Soccer

Women have been playing soccer for centuries. Unfortunately, for a long time, they did not receive the support that the men did. In fact, many countries, including Brazil and England, banned women from playing the sport during parts of the last century. While FIFA held the inaugural men's World Cup in 1930, the first FIFA Women's World Cup did not occur until 1991—sixty-one years later!

But despite all the obstacles, women's soccer has grown significantly since 1991. In the thirty-two years between the inaugural Women's World Cup and the most recent edition of the tournament in 2023, overall attendance went from slightly over 500,000 attendees in 1991 to nearly 2 million. That's an increase of about 1.5 million! In the United States, the National Women's Soccer League has seen a steady increase in average attendance over the last decade, going from just over 5,000 spectators per match in 2015 to over 11,000 in 2024.

It's not just attendance that's growing. A 2024 FIFA report discovered that the global number of women and girls enrolled in organized soccer had increased by 25 percent since 2019, reaching 16.6 million people. If you haven't watched a women's soccer game, it's time to join the fun!

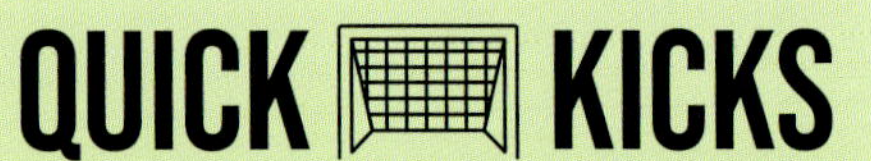

American Kristine Lilly holds the record for most international caps (354) in women's soccer. She played from 1987 to 2010.

FIFA's Continued Fight Against Racism

Soccer is a game for *everyone*. But sometimes, players have been treated unfairly because of their skin color, background, or where they're from. That's called racism, and it's a serious problem that has happened in soccer—especially from some fans during games.

In some matches, fans have shouted mean things or made rude gestures toward players. This has happened to famous players like Vinícius Jr., Bukayo Saka, and Antonio Rüdiger, and it's made many people speak out and demand change.

FIFA has been working to stop racism since 1960. They've made rules that say racism and discrimination are not allowed, and they've created special teams and events to teach people about fairness and respect. In 2013, FIFA started the Taskforce Against Racism and Discrimination to come up with new ways to make soccer safer and kinder. They also work with big groups like the United Nations to spread messages of equality.

Today, if racism happens during a game, referees can pause or even stop the match. Fans who act badly can be banned from stadiums, and teams can be punished too. Because soccer isn't just a sport—it's a celebration where *everyone* should feel welcome, safe, and proud to play.

Mini Quiz: Global Impact

How have the players in this section made impacts outside the pitch? Let's see if you remember!

1. What was the name of the youth soccer team Stanley Matthews established in Soweto during apartheid?

- **A.** Matthews United
- **B.** Soweto Stars
- **C.** Stan's Men

2. Which organization did Pelé start in 2018 to fight against poverty and hunger?

- **A.** The Pelé Foundation
- **B.** Global Goals Initiative
- **C.** Soccer for Peace

3. What major honor did Megan Rapinoe receive in 2022 for her advocacy work?

- **A.** Nobel Peace Prize
- **B.** Presidential Medal of Freedom
- **C.** FIFA Humanitarian Award

Bonus Question

When did FIFA hold the first Women's World Cup?

A. 1960 **B.** 1991 **C.** 2000

Answer Key: C., A., B., Bonus: B.

FFF
FRANCE-CROATIE
15 JUILLET 2018
10

Chapter 9

Become the Next Soccer Legend

Many of the players in this book began as young kids curious about the sport, just like you, before embarking on the journeys that took them to their professional careers. Along the way, they faced different types of struggles, such as a lack of opportunities, having to improve, or even overcoming injuries. Through it all, they persevered to become the type of athlete other players dream of being.

As you begin to play soccer and face your own challenges, don't let those challenges deter you. Instead, view them as defenders that you need to dribble past to score—or, in your case, reach—your goals. Dream big, practice, and continue to work hard to become the best player you can be. Remember: practice makes perfect. Who knows? One day, you might even end up in a book about the best soccer players of all time!

QUICK KICKS

A long time ago, soccer balls weren't smooth and bouncy like today—they were made from pig bladders! Yes, the squishy part inside a pig. Thankfully, rubber came along and saved the day. Now, soccer balls go through many tests to make sure they bounce just right, weigh the perfect amount, and don't soak up water like a sponge!

Kylian Mbappé with the FIFA World Cup trophy after France beat Croatia in 2018.

The Magic of Numbers!

Did you know that in soccer, the number ten jersey holds a special place in the game? It's not just a number—it's a symbol of greatness and great responsibility! Some of the most amazing players in the sport wore the number ten, including Pelé, Maradona, and Messi.

Traditionally, the number ten is given to the team's most creative and gifted player, generally a playmaker (the brain of the team) or an attacking midfielder. The players who wear the number ten have to make sure they create scoring chances, lead attacks, and inspire their teammates. Usually when you see someone wearing number ten, you know they're one of the best players in their team.

So next time you're picking a jersey, think about what number tells your story. Maybe you'll be the next soccer legend! And remember—whether you wear the number ten or ninety-nine, what matters most is having fun!

OTHER IMPORTANT NUMBERS

The number ten isn't the only number with a special meaning in soccer—lots of jersey numbers are linked to certain positions on the team!

ONE: Usually worn by the goalkeeper
TWO: This is the number typically worn by a right back defender
THREE: This number is usually worn by a left back defender
FOUR: Often this number is worn by a center back or defensive midfielder
FIVE: Another number usually worn by the center back
SIX: The number six is often worn by the defensive midfielder
SEVEN: This number is typical for a speedy winger or attacker
EIGHT: Generally, you will see a central midfielder wear this number
NINE: This is the number often chosen for the striker
ELEVEN: Another number usually worn by a speedy winger or attacker

Diego Maradona celebrates the penalty shoot-out victory over Italy in the 1990 FIFA World Cup Semifinal.

adidas
10

Dream Big, Play Hard

Now that you've read about all these amazing soccer players, you're probably ready to jump onto a field and play, or at least watch a game. With so many different teams, you may be wondering how to get started. The first step is to talk to your parents, so you can figure out the best way to begin your soccer journey. Here are a few fun ways to get involved:

Join a local youth team. Soccer is played at every level, and there are many ways to begin playing organized games. If you're a beginner and are looking for something fun with low commitments, you can visit local community centers with your parents and check out recreational leagues. Recreational leagues focus on ensuring everyone gets to play. For a more structured experience, explore joining a soccer academy or travel teams. Academies and travel teams often include tryouts and regular training sessions, making it more of a time commitment, which is perfect for players who want to one day pursue playing in high school or college or having a career in the sport.

Head to the park and play with friends. The beauty of soccer is that it's a simple game that can be played anywhere. If you can't find any organized soccer near you, you can always ask your parents if you can head to a local field, park, or green space with some friends to kick the ball around. You can even play it indoors! Some of the best players began playing soccer after school with their friends in unexpected spaces, which helped them refine their skills and forced them to get creative!

Support your local team. There may be a professional or a semiprofessional team near you. Find a local team and ask your parents if you can go watch a game at the stadium with them. In addition to the excitement of watching the game and seeing the players in person, the crowd will shout plenty of chants to keep you engaged the whole time. Not only is going to a soccer match a great way to spend an afternoon with family and friends, you can learn a lot from watching professional soccer players up close. If you don't have any soccer clubs near you, you can always go support your local high school or college soccer teams.

Marcus Rashford of Manchester United celebrates scoring a goal during the Premier League match between Manchester United and Wolverhampton Wanderers.

adidas
CHEVROLET

Glossary

Here is a list of some important terms to know in the world of soccer.

Assist: The pass made to set up a goal.

Ballon d'Or: A trophy given to the best player in the world by *France Football* magazine. It is considered the highest individual honor in soccer.

Brace: When a player scores two goals in a single game.

Cap: When a player represents the national team, it is said the player has earned a cap.

Champions League: Typically refers to UEFA's annual premier club competition, which is considered by many the most prestigious title at club level. CAF also has a Champions League.

Copa América: CONMEBOL's continental tournament at the international level. It is the oldest international soccer tournament.

Copa Libertadores: CONMEBOL's annual premier club competition.

Corner kick: A kick awarded to the attacking team when the defending team plays the ball over the end line its goal is on. The kick is taken from the corner flag.

Cross: A long pass from out wide intended for a player inside the penalty box of the opposite team.

Cup: The prize given for winning a league or tournament; sometimes refers to the World Cup itself.

Derby: A rivalry between two teams.

Domestic: Refers to a national league or tournament.

Double: Winning two trophies in one season.

Dribble: When a player moves the ball up and down the field with his feet, including past opponents.

Euro: UEFA's continental tournament at the international level.

European Golden Shoe: Award given to the highest scorer in European soccer.

Formation: The way a team sets up on the field, which affects the tactics it uses.

Free kick: A kick awarded to a team that suffers a foul. These can be direct, meaning the kicker can attempt to score from a direct kick, or indirect, in which case the ball must be touched by another player before attempting a goal.

Goal: When the ball crosses the goal line and touches the back of the net, resulting in a point for one of the teams.

Goal kick: Kick given to the defending team when the other team plays the ball over the endline it is attacking. It's taken from inside the penalty box.

Golden Ball: Award given to the best player in a tournament. The second-best player is sometimes given a Silver Ball, and the third-best player earns a Bronze Ball.

Golden Boot: Award given to the highest scorer in a tournament.

Golden Glove: Award given to the best goalkeeper in a tournament.

Handball: When a player touches the ball with their hand, the ball is given to the other team for either a free kick or a penalty kick.

Hat trick: When a player scores three goals in a single match.

Header: When a player plays the ball with their head, either to score or clear the ball.

Loan: When a player plays temporarily for a certain team they are not contracted to play for.

Lob: A high kick that sends the ball over other players—like defenders or the goalie—and lands near a teammate or the goal.

Match: A soccer game.

Offside: A player is in an offside position if any part of their head, body, or feet is in the opponent's goal line excluding the halfway line, and if any part of their head, body, or feet is nearer to the opponent's goal line than both the ball and the second to last opponent.

Penalty kick: A kick taken from the penalty spot—12 yards from the goal—as a result of a foul or a handball inside the penalty box.

Pitch: Another word for soccer field.

Possession: When a team has the ball during a match.

Quadruple: When a team wins four trophies in a season, including a treble.

Set piece: A set piece refers to a kick from a stopped ball, such as a free kick or corner kick.

Sextuple: When a team wins six trophies in a season, including a treble.

Shutouts: When a team goes an entire match without giving up a goal. This is sometimes also called a clean sheet.

Tiki-taka: Style of play that focuses on possession and quick, short passes. Made famous by Barcelona and Spain's national team.

Total football: Style of play that focuses on the idea that any player can play in any position on the field at any given time. Popularized by Ajax and the Netherlands' national team.

Treble: When a team wins three trophies in a season, specifically the league, a domestic cup, and a continental trophy

World Cup: FIFA's premier international soccer tournament that is held every four years. It is considered the highest honor in sports.

World Cup Champions

Winning a World Cup is the dream of every player who has ever had the opportunity to represent their country. Playing in the World Cup wearing your nation's colors is an incredible honor, but to win that shiny trophy for your country? That's the stuff of legends. There have been twenty-two editions of the Men's World Cup and nine editions of the Women's World Cup, with only eleven nations winning a title in those tournaments. Below is a list of the countries that have managed to raise the trophy, along with some interesting facts about them.

Men's World Cup Champions

Brazil: 1958, 1962, 1970, 1994, 2002

Brazil is the only team to have played in every World Cup, winning the competition a record five times, as well as in back-to-back editions (1958, 1962).

Germany: 1954, 1974, 1990, 2014

Germany has reached the World Cup Final on eight occasions, winning the trophy four times. Germany won its first three World Cups as West Germany, before reunifying with East Germany in late 1990.

Italy: 1934, 1938, 1982, 2006

Italy was the first European nation to win the World Cup and is one of only two countries to win the competition in back-to-back editions (1934, 1938).

Argentina: 1978, 1986, 2022

Argentina is currently the reigning World Cup champion, and has won each of the last three major international trophies it has played for, including the last two Copa América titles (2021, 2024).

France: 1998, 2018

Following its first World Cup victory in 1998, France went on to win the Euro 2000.

Uruguay: 1930, 1950

Uruguay was the first nation to host the World Cup, as well as the first to win the prized trophy.

England: 1966

England won the World Cup the same year they hosted the tournament.

Spain: 2010

Between 2008 and 2012, Spain won every major continental and international title at the senior level, including two Euros (2008, 2012).

Women's World Cup Champions

US: 1991, 1999, 2015, 2019

The US Women's National Team won the inaugural Women's World Cup in 1991 and has won twice as many World Cups as the next closest team.

Germany: 2003, 2007

Between 2001 and 2009, the German women's national team won every major continental and international title at the senior level, including three Women's Euros (2001, 2005, 2009).

Norway: 1995

Norway was the first European team to win the Women's World Cup.

Japan: 2011

Japan's women's national team remains the only Asian team to win a World Cup for either gender at the senior level.

Spain: 2023

The reigning Women's World Cup champions, Spain's squad features some of the best current players.

Hometown Rivalries

Derbies, Clásicos, and More

Soccer, like any other sport, has its share of rivalries that have developed over the years. A match between rival teams is called a "derby" game in English, or a *clásico* in Spanish. Derby matches are typically between clubs from the same city or region, as they play to determine the dominant team in a city or in a country! Below are some of the most famous club rivalries in soccer as well as their nicknames:

- Boca Juniors and River Plate (Argentina): *Superclásico*
- Liverpool and Manchester United (England): The North West Derby
- Lazio and Roma (Italy): *Il Derby della Capitale*
- Barcelona and Real Madrid (Spain): *El Clásico*
- Fenerbahce and Galatasaray (Türkiye): The Intercontinental Derby

Soccer Organizations

Asian Football Confederation (AFC): https://www.the-afc.com.

Confederation of African Football (CAF): https://www.cafonline.com.

Confederation of North, Central America, and Caribbean Association Football (Concacaf): https://www.concacaf.com.

Fédération Internationale de Football Association (FIFA): https://www.fifa.com.

International Federation of Football History & Statistics (IFFHS): https://www.iffhs.com.

International Olympics Committee (IOC): https://www.olympics.com.

Oceania Football Confederation: https://www.oceaniafootball.com.

South American Football Confederation (CONMEBOL): https://www.conmebol.com.

The International Football Association Board (IFAB): https://www.theifab.com.

Union of European Football Associations (UEFA): https://www.uefa.com.

Soccer Clubs

AC Milan: https://www.acmilan.com.

Ajax: https://www.ajax.nl.

Al Ahli Dubai: http://www.shabab-ae.com.

Anzhi Makhachkala: http://www.fc-anji.ru.

Arsenal FC: https://www.arsenal.com.

AS Monaco: https://www.asmonaco.com.

AS Nancy: https://www.asnl.net.

AS Roma: https://www.asroma.com.

Atalanta: https://www.atalanta.it.

Atlas: https://www.atlasfc.com.mx.

FC Barcelona: https://www.fcbarcelona.com.

Bayer Leverkusen: https://www.bayer04.de.

Bayern Munich: https://fcbayern.com.

Boca Juniors: https://www.bocajuniors.com.ar.

Borussia Mönchengladbach: https://www.borussia.de.

Brasileirão: https://brasileirao.com.br.

Brescia: https://www.bresciacalcio.it.

Brøndby: https://brondby.com.

Bundesliga (Germany): https://www.bundesliga.com.

CA River Plate: https://www.cariverplate.com.ar.

Celtic: https://www.celticfc.com.

C.F. Monterrey: https://www.rayados.com.

Chelsea: https://www.chelseafc.com.

Chicago Fire: https://www.chicagofirefc.com.

Chicago Red Stars: https://www.chicagoredstars.com.

Colo Colo: https://www.colocolo.cl.

Colorado Rapids: https://www.coloradorapids.com.

D.C. United: https://www.dcunited.com.

Deportivo Cali: https://www.deportivocali.co.

Dunstable Town: https://www.dunstabletownfc.co.uk.

Dynamo Kyiv: https://fcdynamo.com.

Emelec: https://www.csemelec.com.

English Premier League: https://www.premierleague.com.

Eredivisie (Netherlands): https://www.eredivisie.nl.

Espanyol: https://www.rcdespanyol.co.

Everton: https://www.evertonfc.com.

Feyenoord: https://www.feyenoord.com.

Fiorentina: https://www.acffiorentina.com.

Flamengo: https://www.flamengo.com.br.

Fluminense: https://www.fluminense.com.br.

FSV Frankfurt: https://www.fsv-frankfurt.de.
Fulham: https://www.fulhamfc.com.
Grêmio: https://gremio.net.
Groningen: https://www.fcgroningen.nl.
Hamburger SV: https://www.hsv.de.
Hellas Verona: https://www.hellasverona.it.
Herning Fremad: https://www.herningfremad.dk.
Hibernian: https://www.hibernianfc.co.uk.
Huracán: https://www.huracan.com.ar.
Inter Milan: https://www.inter.it.
Italian Serie A: https://www.legaseriea.it.
Juventude: https://www.juventude.com.br.
Juventus: https://www.juventus.com.
Kashiwa Reysol: https://www.reysol.co.jp.
LaLiga (Spain): https://www.laliga.com.
León: https://www.clubleon.mx.
Ligue 1 (France): https://www.ligue1.com.
Liverpool FC: https://www.liverpoolfc.com.
Major League Soccer (MLS): https://www.mlssoccer.com.
Manchester City: https://www.mancity.com.
Manchester United: https://www.manutd.com.
Millonarios: https://www.millonarios.com.co.
Montpellier: https://www.mhscfoot.com.
Napoli: https://www.sscnapoli.it.
National Women's Soccer League (NWSL):
https://www.nwslsoccer.com.
Newell's Old Boys: https://www.newellsoldboys.com.ar.
New York Cosmos: https://www.nycosmos.com.
Olympiacos FC: https://www.olympiacos.org.
Orlando Pride: https://www.orlandocitysc.com/pride.
Paris Saint-Germain: https://en.psg.fr.
Parma Calcio 1913: https://parmacalcio1913.com.
Portland Thorns: https://www.timbers.com/thornsfc.
PSV Eindhoven: https://www.psv.nl.
Qatar SC: https://www.qatarsc.qa.
Querétaro FC: https://www.clubqueretaro.com.
Rayo Vallecano: https://www.rayovallecano.es.
RB Leipzig: https://rbleipzig.com.
RC Celta de Vigo: https://rccelta.es.
RC Lens: https://www.rclens.fr.
RC Strasbourg Alsace: https://www.rcstrasbourgalsace.fr.
Real Madrid CF: https://www.realmadrid.com.
Real Sociedad: https://www.realsociedad.eus.
Real Valladolid: https://www.realvalladolid.es.
Real Zaragoza: https://www.realzaragoza.com.
RSC Anderlecht: https://www.rsca.be.
Sampdoria: https://www.sampdoria.it.
Santos FC: https://www.santosfc.com.br.
San Jose Earthquakes: https://www.sjearthquakes.com.
Seattle Sounders FC: https://www.soundersfc.com.
Sevilla FC: https://www.sevillafc.es.
Sunderland AFC: https://www.safc.com.
Swansea City AFC: https://www.swanseacity.com.
Sydney FC: https://www.sydneyfc.com.
Tottenham Hotspur FC: https://www.tottenhamhotspur.com.
Udinese Calcio: https://www.udinese.it.
Umeå IK: https://www.umeaik.se.

Select References

Books

Fishman, Jon M. *Soccer's G.O.A.T.: Pelé, Lionel Messi, and More*. Lerner Publications, 2020. https://cml.bibliocommons.com/v2/record/S105C3241538.

Funk, Joe, ed. *Sports Illustrated Kids Big Book of WHO All-Stars*. Triumph Books LLC, 2021. https://cml.bibliocommons.com/v2/record/S105C4120421.

Gifford, Clive. *The Kingfisher Soccer Encyclopedia*. Kingfisher, 2018. https://cml.bibliocommons.com/v2/record/S105C2943141.

Hawkes, Chris, ed. *Goal!: Soccer as You've Never Seen It Before*. Dorling Kindersley Limited, a Penguin Random House Company, 2017.

Hewson, Anthony K. *GOATs of Soccer*. SportsZone, a division of Abdo, 2022. https://cml.bibliocommons.com/v2/record/S105C3640436.

Huddlestone, Emma. *Legends of Women's Soccer*. Press Room Editions LLC, 2021. https://cml.bibliocommons.com/v2/record/S105C3669942.

Jökulsson, Illugi. *U.S. Women's Team: Soccer Champions!* Abbeville Press Publishers, 2015. https://cml.bibliocommons.com/v2/record/S105C2014991.

Killion, Ann. *Champions of Women's Soccer*. Philomel Books, 2018. https://cml.bibliocommons.com/v2/record/S105C2953559.

Skene, Rona, ed. *Everything You Need to Know About Soccer!* DK Publishing, 2022. https://cml.bibliocommons.com/v2/record/S105C3719237.

Walters, Meg. *World Cup Women*. Sky Pony Press, 2019. https://cml.bibliocommons.com/v2/record/S105C3250444.

Web Articles

Adgate, Brad. "A Conversation with Jessica Berman, Commissioner, NWSL." Forbes, October 1, 2024. Accessed April 22, 2025. https://www.forbes.com/sites/bradadgate/2024/10/01/a-conversation-with-jessica-berman-commissioner-nwsl/.

BBC News. "George Weah Sworn in as Liberia's President." BBC News, November 6, 2017. https://www.bbc.com/news/world-africa-41824586.

BBC Sport. "He Is the Greatest Ambassador." BBC Sport. Accessed August 18, 2025. https://www.bbc.com/sport/football/articles/cx2xlk74llno.

"British Goalkeeper Tom King Breaks Record for Longest Football Goal." Guinness World Records, January 21, 2021. Accessed January 31, 2025. https://www.guinnessworldrecords.com/news/2021/1/british-goalkeeper-tom-king-breaks-record-for-longest-football-goal-646285.

CIES Football Observatory. "Estimated Transfer Values of Football Players Worldwide." Accessed February 28, 2025. https://football-observatory.com/IMG/sites/mr/mr68/en/.

FIFA. Diversity and Anti Discrimination at FIFA. ICSSPE. Accessed March 4, 2025. https://www.icsspe.org/system/files/FIFA%20-%20Diversity%20and%20Anti-discrimination%20at%20FIFA.pdf.

FIFA. "FIFA Releases Global Women's Football Landscape Survey Report." Accessed January 19, 2025. https://inside.fifa.com/womens-football/news/fifa-releases-global-womens-football-landscape-survey.

FIFA. FIFA Women's World Cup 2023: Tournament Recap – A World Cup of Firsts. Accessed May 4, 2025. https://inside.fifa.com/tournament-organisation/fifa-womens-world-cup-2023-tournament-recap#a-world-cup-of-firsts.

FIFA. FIFA World Cup Qatar 2022 in Numbers. FIFA Annual Report 2022. Accessed March 24, 2025. https://publications.fifa.com/en/annual-report-2022/tournaments-and-events/fifa-world-cup-quatar-2022/fifa-world-cup-qatar-2022-in-numbers/.

FIFA. Technical Report: FIFA Women's World Cup China PR 1991 – Part 2. Archived December 27, 2011. Accessed January 27, 2025.

https://web.archive.org/web/20111227003624/http://www.fifa.com/mm/document/afdeveloping/technicaldevp/50/08/19/wwc%5f91%5ftr%5fpart2%5f260.pdf.

"George Weah." IFFHS Legends. Accessed April 4, 2025. https://iffhs.com/legends/29.

Houston Dynamo FC. "Five Things to Know about UNAM Pumas." Houston Dynamo FC, March 2, 2022. https://www.houstondynamofc.com/houstondash/news/five-things-to-know-about-unam-pumas.

Keh, Andrew. "How Many Miles Do Soccer Players Run in a Game?" Sports Illustrated. Accessed January 23, 2025. https://www.si.com/soccer/how-many-miles-do-soccer-players-run-in-a-game.

"Marcus Rashford: From United Star to Hunger Hero." Manchester Evening News. Archived January 14, 2021. Accessed January 30, 2025. https://web.archive.org/web/20210114153512/https:/www.manchestereveningnews.co.uk/news/greater-manchester-news/manchester-united-star-marcus-rashford-17098086

"Marcus Rashford: Free School Meals Campaign." BBC News, June 16, 2020. Accessed March 6, 2025. https://www.bbc.com/news/uk-53065806.

"Matthews, the Original No 7: The Story of When Sir Stanley Took on Apartheid." The Times. Accessed March 12, 2025. https://www.thetimes.com/sport/football/article/matthews-the-original-no-7-the-story-of-when-sir-stanley-took-on-apartheid-zxhrjc0Oh.

"Megan Rapinoe: Her Undeniable Impact." U.S. Soccer. September 2023. Accessed February 21, 2025. https://www.ussoccer.com/stories/2023/09/megan-rapinoe-undeniable-impact.

Ogden, Mark. "Marcus Rashford Embraces Man United Leadership Role and Giving Back." ESPN. Archived January 14, 2021. Accessed February 18, 2025. https://web.archive.org/web/20210114153514/https://www.espn.co.uk/football/manchester-united/story/3998258/marcus-rashford-embraces-man-united-leadership-role-and-giving-back-to-the-city-he-loves.

Pelak, Cynthia Fabrizio. "Negotiating Gendered Discourses: Women's National Soccer in South Africa." South African Historical Journal 73, no. 1 (2021). Accessed May 1, 2025. https://www.tandfonline.com/doi/abs/10.1080/02582473.2021.1875032.

PlayerData. "Positional Variations in Match Day Distance." PlayerData Blog. Accessed May 5, 2025. https://www.playerdata.com/blog/positional-variations-in-match-day-distance.

"President Biden Signs Equal Pay Bill into Law." U.S. Senate Committee on Commerce, Science, & Transportation. Accessed February 14, 2025. https://www.commerce.senate.gov/2023/1/president-biden-signs-cantwell-capito-equal-pay-bill-into-law.

"S.2333 – Equal Pay for Team USA Act of 2022." Congress.gov. Accessed January 11, 2025. https://www.congress.gov/bill/117th-congress/senate-bill/2333.

Scottish Football Association. Scottish Football: History of the Game. Archived March 8, 2005. Accessed January 10, 2025. https://web.archive.org/web/20050308172042/http:/www.scottishfa.co.uk/scottish_football.cfm?curpageid=409

Stanford Magazine. "The Salah Effect." Stanford Magazine. Accessed August 18, 2025. https://stanfordmag.org/contents/the-salah-effect.

Statista. "Number of Spectators at Football World Cups from 1930 to 2022." Accessed February 5, 2025. https://www.statista.com/statistics/264441/number-of-spectators-at-football-world-cups-since-1930/.

Taylor, Louise. "'No One Comes Close': Sam Kerr Wins English Football's Player of the Year." The Guardian, April 30, 2022. Accessed April 18, 2025. https://www.theguardian.com/football/2022/apr/30/no-one-comes-close-sam-kerr-wins-english-footballs-player-of-year.

"The Story of Sir Stanley Matthews and Apartheid-Era South Africa." BBC News. Accessed March 26, 2025. http://news.bbc.co.uk/local/stoke/hi/people_and_places/history/newsid_8775000/8775869.stm.

UN Women. "Marta Vieira da Silva." UN Women. Accessed August 18, 2025. https://www.unwomen.org/en/partnerships/goodwill-ambassadors/marta-vieira-da-silva.

"USSF and National Team Unions Agree to Historic CBAs." U.S. Soccer. May 2022. Accessed April 9, 2025. https://www.ussoccer.com/stories/2022/05/ussf-womens-and-mens-national-team-unions-agree-to-historic-collective-bargaining-agreements.

"USWNT, US Soccer Sign Historic Equal Pay Agreement." Just Women's Sports. Accessed May 3, 2025. https://justwomenssports.com/reads/uswnt-cba-signing-us-soccer-equal-pay/.

Image Credits

Page 2: © Stefan Matzke - sampics/Getty
Page 4: © Aurelien Meunier - PSG/Getty
Page 6: © Clive Mason/Getty
Page 16: © Marco Iacobucci Epp/Shutterstock
Page 18: © Neal Simpson - EMPICS/Getty
Page 20: © Hulton Deutsch/Getty
Page 24: © Thierry Orban/Getty
Page 26: © TORU YAMANAKA/Getty
Page 27: © Bob Thomas/Getty
Page 29: © Alberto Sereno/Getty
Page 31: © Alex Livesey/Getty
Page 32: © Stuart Franklin - FIFA/Getty
Page 34: © Rich Barnes/Getty
Page 37: © Peter Robinson - EMPICS/Getty
Page 38: © Bob Thomas/Getty
Page 39: © CARLO BARONCINI/Getty
Page 45: © Harriet Lander - The FA/Getty
Page 50: © Denis Doyle/Getty
Page 53: © STF/Getty
Page 55: © Bob Thomas/Getty
Page 56: © Jerome Prevost/Getty
Page 57: © John Berry/Getty
Page 61: © David Cannon/Getty
Page 64: © David Ramos/Getty
Page 65: © Michael Regan/Getty
Page 72: © David Ramos/Getty
Page 73: © Quinn Rooney/Getty
Page 75: © ph.FAB/Shutterstock
Page 76: © Alexandra Beier - FIFA/Getty
Page 77: © Clive Brunskill/Getty
Page 80: © Brad Smith/ISI Photos/USSF/Getty
Page 82: © Andy Lyons/Getty
Page 83: © Hulton Archive/Getty
Page 85: © Focus On Sport/Getty
Page 86: © Central Press/Getty
Page 88: © Tony Marshall - EMPICS/Getty
Page 89: © Neal Simpson - EMPICS/Getty
Page 93: © Al Messerschmidt/Getty
Page 96: © Claudio Villa/ Grazia Neri/Getty
Page 97: © Jeff Gross/Getty
Page 99: © Giuseppe Bellini/Getty
Page 100: © FRANCK FIFE/Getty
Page 101: © Ben Radford/Getty
Page 107: © Patrick Smith - FIFA/Getty
Page 108: © Icon Sportswire/Getty
Page 109: © Bongarts/Getty
Page 110: © Ringo Chiu/Shutterstock
Page 111: © Matthew Peters/Getty
Page 113: © Stefan Constantin 22/Shutterstock
Page 116: © Ververidis Vasilis/Shutterstock
Page 117: © Marco Iacobucci Epp/Shutterstock
Page 120: © Minas Panagiotakis/Getty
Page 122: © Adam Davy - EMPICS/Getty
Page 123: © Alex Grimm/Getty
Page 124: © Peter Robinson - EMPICS/Getty
Page 126: © Shaun Botterill/Getty
Page 127: © Kevin C. Cox - FIFA/Getty
Page 128: © Sportsphoto/Allstar/Getty
Page 130: © Michael Regan/Getty
Page 135: © Jan Kruger - FIFA/Getty
Page 136: © Michael Steele/Getty
Page 138: © Central Press/Getty
Page 139: © Rolls Press/Popperfoto/Getty
Page 144: © NurPhoto/Getty
Page 147: © Getty Images
Page 149: © Ash Donelon/Getty

Acknowledgments

First, I would like to thank all three of my parents: My mom, Patricia Deeb, who has always been my biggest cheerleader; my dad, Douglas Mojica, for teaching me about the history of soccer; and my dad, Walter Deeb, for driving to high schools all over Northeast Ohio to watch me play. Next, I would like to thank my wife, Sara, for being so loving and supportive.

I would also like to acknowledge Jorge Martinez, Danielle Coombs, and Gary Moody, the best mentors I could ask for, and all of my soccer colleagues and friends who were kind enough to serve as a sounding board as I began to write.

I'm especially thankful to Quarto Kids—Rage, Keyla, and the graphic design team—for allowing me to write a book about the sport I love so dearly. When they approached me to assemble a list of legendary players, they probably had no idea that I've been arranging and rearranging this list my whole life.

Finally, thank you, the reader, for choosing to read this book. May you enjoy reading it as much as I enjoyed writing it.

About the Author

CARLOS MOJICA is a bilingual communications professional who collects soccer shirts. Born in El Salvador and raised in Ohio, he fell in love with soccer by watching the "original" Ronaldo dominate defenses. Carlos learned world geography by memorizing different soccer clubs around the world. His professional experience includes working for the Columbus Crew and the National Premier Soccer League, as well as collaborating with Major League Soccer and Concacaf on various high-profile events. He lives in Columbus with his wife, Sara, an ESL teacher who is as passionate as she is caring.

First published in 2026 by becker&mayer!kids,
an imprint of The Quarto Group,
135 West 36th Street, 13th Floor, New York, NY 10018, USA
(212) 779-4972 www.Quarto.com

EEA Representation, WTS Tax d.o.o.,
Žanova ulica 3, 4000 Kranj, Slovenia.
www.wts-tax.si

10 9 8 7 6 5 4 3 2 1

ISBN: 978-1-57715-709-0

Digital edition published in 2026
eISBN: 978-1-57715-710-6

Library of Congress Control Number: 2025945768

Group Publisher: Rage Kindelsperger
Creative Director: Laura Drew
Managing Editor: Cara Donaldson
Editor: Keyla Pizarro-Hernández
Text: Carlos Mojica
Art Director: Scott Richardson
Cover and Interior Design: Foltz Design

Printed in Huizhou City, Guangdong, China TT122025

LEXILE

Lexile®: 1200L